Discovering Main Street

Discovering Main Street

Travel Adventures
in Small Towns of the Northwest

Foster Church

Oregon State University Press
Corvallis

Discovering Main Street has its origins as a monthly column for the Travel section of *The Sunday Oregonian,* a Portland newspaper. The intention was to visit small towns and write about them as tourist destinations. Although the essays in this book differ from the columns, the theme remains the same.

The paper in this book meets the guidelines for permanence and durability of the Committee on Production Guidelines for Book Longevity of the Council on Library Resources and the minimum requirements of the American National Standard for Permanence of Paper for Printed Library Materials Z39.48-1984.

Library of Congress Cataloging-in-Publication Data
Church, Foster.
  Discovering main street : travel adventures in small towns of the Northwest / by Foster Church.
    p. cm.
  Includes index.
  ISBN 978-0-87071-587-7 (alk. paper)
  1. Northwest, Pacific--Description and travel. 2. Northwest, Pacific--History, Local. 3. Cities and towns--Northwest, Pacific. 4. City and town life--Northwest, Pacific. 5. Northwest, Pacific--Social life and customs. 6. Northwest, Pacific--Guidebooks. I. Title.
  F852.3.C49 2010
  979.5--dc22
                                        2010007212

First published in 2010 by Oregon State University Press
Printed in the United States of America

 Oregon State University Press
121 The Valley Library
Corvallis OR 97331-4501
541-737-3166 • fax 541-737-3170
http://oregonstate.edu/dept/press

Dedication

Dedicated to Sue Hobart, who as travel editor of *The Oregonian* championed, encouraged, and edited the author's travel column, *Oregon Offtrack* (and *Washington Offtrack*), which provided the basis for this book

Contents

Introduction 8

Willamette Valley 11
Estacada 13
Mt. Angel 17
Dallas 20
Scio/Stayton/Sublimity 24
Brownsville 27
Harrisburg 32
Cottage Grove 36
Oakridge 39

Oregon Coast 43
Clatskanie 45
Garibaldi 48
Oceanside 51
Toledo 55
Reedsport 58
Charleston 61
Myrtle Point 64
Powers 67
Gold Beach 70

Southern Oregon 73
Sutherlin/Oakland 75
Wolf Creek 79
Gold Hill/Rogue River 83
Shady Cove 87
Cave Junction/Takilma 90
Christmas Valley 94
Paisley 98
Lakeview 102

Eastern Oregon 107
Moro 109
Fossil 112
Heppner 116
Spray 119
Mitchell 122
John Day/Canyon City 125
Prairie City 129
Sumpter 133
Milton-Freewater 136
Troy 140
Enterprise 143
Elgin 147
Halfway 151
Jordan Valley 154
Burns 158
McDermitt 161
Fields 165

Southern Washington 169
South Bend 171
Ilwaco 174
White Salmon 178
Lyle 182
Dayton 185

Epilogue 189
Index 191

Introduction

This book celebrates the small towns of the Northwest as places to spend time and explore. Usually, we pass through them on the road to someplace else.

As tourists, most of us are passive. We visit a place because we know what it offers: a great museum, a fabulous beach, famous restaurants, or magnificent natural surroundings. Visiting small towns as a tourist calls for a different mindset. Their attractions aren't well known; they have to be searched out. It's do-it-yourself tourism.

Enjoying a small town is more than seeing the sights. Just as important is absorbing the culture of the place: having breakfast in a café, dropping in on local meetings, attending a rodeo, a parade, an ice cream social, a high-school sporting event, or a little theater production. The enjoyment is also in talking to people: the druggist, the bartender, the librarian, the motel desk clerk, the volunteers in the historical museum and the Chamber of Commerce. Small-town people are proud of their homes and eager to share them.

I define small towns loosely. In this book, they range from Fields, with a population of thirteen, to Dallas, where over fifteen thousand people reside. Usually, I avoid towns that are already well-known tourist attractions. This means that I have excluded most coastal small towns. My most basic criterion for choosing a town to write about is that it offers overnight accommodation. This can be a motel, a hotel, a bed-and-breakfast, or even an apartment upstairs from a local restaurant. For the most part, I have found these hostelries clean, well equipped, and centrally located. Only once have I had to refrain from writing about a place because the lodging was so bad. I often recommend lodging and restaurants in this book, but I have made no effort to be definitive. For the most part, travelers must find these places themselves.

Here is the way I recommend exploring a small town:

A challenge when entering a small town for the first time is a sinking feeling. The place can look desolate, worn, and dusty. A day or two later, it will look completely different, so resist the urge to turn around.

My first stop is usually the Chamber of Commerce or the visitors bureau. Most small towns have them, and while they are not the last word, they can acquaint you with the basics. I stock up on brochures, maps, and other written information. I usually ask for the name of the town historian or a person who has lived in the town for a long time. I ask where people go for breakfast in the morning and where I will find the best view of the town. I also ask for a list of the top ten things to see or do in the town and environs.

Next I buy a copy of the local newspaper. Most small towns have at least a weekly. Then I go to a café for lunch or coffee and read the paper front to back. These papers capture the flavor of the town and usually contain a calendar of events that tells what's going on—perhaps a rodeo, a recital, or cowboy church on Sunday morning.

9

If a town offers neither a visitors bureau nor a newspaper, check out billboards in the library, outside the grocery store, or in the local tavern, where special events are often posted. Also, find out if anything special is happening at the high school. Schools are the heart of a small town, and nearly everyone attends basketball and football games.

Find the best view of the town. Sometimes it's at the top of a nearby mountain, in other places it's just a knoll. But the view places the town in its environment. Also discover the best hikes and the finest rivers, creeks, waterfalls, forest glades, stony canyons, and scenic drives.

Satisfy your curiosity. You have time in a small town to nose around and learn about things that intrigue you. These can be an antique car parked at the side of the road, a huge piece of machinery, a grain elevator, or a windmill. Once you find the owner or the person responsible, you will be pleased at their willingness to answer your questions and show you around.

If there is a significant manufacturing business in a town, find out if it offers tours. I have been fascinated by tours of a recreational vehicle factory, a grain elevator, and a manufacturer of metal detectors.

Find gathering places. Most towns have a café where people meet for coffee and conversation in the morning. At night, some also drop by the local bar for a drink or seek out karaoke on Friday and Saturday nights. Bars are good places to people watch and sometimes they capture the spirit of the town. The same is true for church services, particularly if they are held in a historic building or if religion is an important part of the town's culture. A service in a nineteenth-century church can transport you back a hundred years.

Hang loose. You are there to enjoy. A sense of drift in a small town isn't a bad thing. Freed of a rigid schedule, you can pick up an interesting string and find out where it leads.

Willamette Valley

Willamette Valley

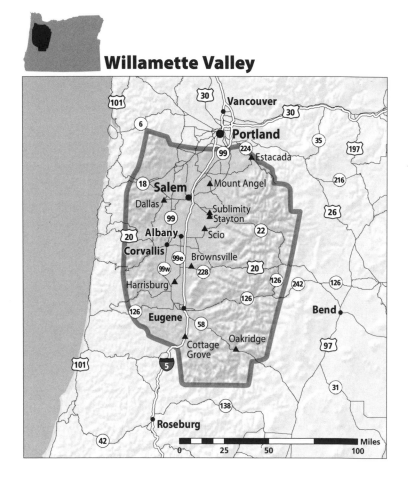

Estacada

2,700

The Road: The most scenic way of entering or leaving Estacada
is to take Forest Service Road 46 north from Detroit and
continue on Oregon 224 to Estacada; however, this route is
often dangerous or impassable from early fall to late spring. A
more direct route from Portland is Oregon 224.

People don't necessarily visit Estacada for its own sake; they
come to play in the Clackamas River, which flows through
town like green silk. Despite its glorious location on the edge
of river and forest, the town has suffered an image problem,
mostly brought on by a stagnant economy following the decline
of the timber industry. Numerous downtown businesses had
closed. It didn't help that Bagby Hot Springs, forty miles
away but closely associated with Estacada, was notorious for
vandalism, assault and drunkenness.

But Estacada has lived down its image. The town has
reinvented itself as an arts center, the downtown is being
spruced up with renovation projects and newly painted murals,
and the raucous scene at Bagby has calmed down, apparently
the result of volunteer efforts.

White settlers began migrating into this valley in the Cascade
foothills in the 1850s, but it got its real start in the early 1900s
when a rail line was extended to support construction of a
nearby dam. Like most small Northwest towns, Estacada
thrived on cutting down trees and making them into lumber
until new federal forest rules reduced the supply. Now, most
of the population commutes thirty-five miles to the Portland
metropolitan area.

Estacada's setting on the edge of the Mount Hood National
Forest is so beautiful that it can cause you to hit the brakes and

13

hope no one is following. The dark woods are said to harbor Sasquatch, which some locals claim to have seen. I talked with a forthright, sensible woman living in a cabin in the woods outside town who related measuring and photographing tracks in the snow of a strange beast with a twelve-inch footprint. Another time, a creature of some kind made large tracks near her cabin and left a terrible stench. The obnoxious odor is said to be a Sasquatch calling card.

My only sighting was out front of Mike's Second Hand Store where Mike keeps a wooden Sasquatch holding the legend, "Shoplifters Will Be Eaten." The store itself is a hairy creature, the biggest secondhand store you'll see outside an auto-wrecking yard. Owner Mike Doolittle says it may be the only secondhand store in the world to have an elevator. It is also, he allows, the second-biggest attraction in Estacada—the first being the Clackamas River. He estimates he might have one hundred thousand items on two floors, stacked, piled, and jammed, but for all this, it is not a mess. Anyone looking for a particular item will have no trouble locating it, and that holds for tools, books, weird appliances long out of production, hideous lamps, and an extensive collection of cookware that follows styles and enthusiasms of the last half century or so. Mike himself is a white-haired, balding man, buoyantly talkative and devoted heart and soul to used stuff. He always has loved scavenging. His parents, he says, used to ground him for packing home junk.

That he puts his secondhand store in the running with the Clackamas River as a tourist draw may show an excess of pride. In the spring and summer, boaters, swimmers, anglers, and whitewater rafters throng the river, but it is lovely at any time of the year, curving through canyons and valleys, foaming over rocks or slowly gliding, its surface a sheet of deep, opaque green.

With time to poke around, there's lots else to see in Estacada and vicinity, including the Springwater Presbyterian Church in the community of Springwater, three miles south of Estacada, the Vila pioneer cemetery, where the gravestones are eloquently inscribed, and near the town of Carver, the Baker log cabin, one of the oldest in Oregon, built in 1856. And for a trip to the bizarre and surreal, there's no better way to end the day than with a drink at Hong's Restaurant and Lounge, once known as the Safari Club. This is a Chinese restaurant with a bar attached—or maybe it should be the other way around.

In the 1970s, the Safari Club was swanky and glamorous, and people came from all over to drink, dine, and dance. Its creator, Glen Park, owned a lumber mill in town that financed his avocation as a big-game hunter. He toured Africa, Central America, and Alaska and brought back magnificent specimens: bear, lion, leopard, cougar, panther, jaguar, cheetah, bobcat, lynx, buffalo, grizzly, bongo, nyala, steenbok, bighorn sheep, wolf, and hyena. Park had these animals—about seventy of them—stuffed and mounted by a Spokane taxidermist and placed in museum-quality dioramas as décor for his restaurant. At one time, you could eat prime rib in sight of tigers and other beasts, stalking, scavenging, and battling to the death. But styles change. The Safari Club switched ownership and local wits found their own names for the place: the So Sorry Club, the Dead Zoo. Park willed the animals to the Tillamook County Pioneer Museum, but it's not clear when or if the museum can find a place for them. The lights have shorted out in most of the display cases. The big cat that leaps snarling above the deserted dance floor is smudged with tobacco smoke and the animals look matted and dusty.

On second thought, perhaps it's not such a great place for a drink. Reality here is distorted enough. Maybe a Coke instead.

15

The Basics: The Red Fox is a clean, basic motel with an excellent location near the Clackamas River. The dining scene is expanding in Estacada, but the Cazadero Inn remains a favorite for its food and river views.

Mt. Angel
3,600

The Road: Coming from north or south, the most efficient way to reach Mt. Angel is take the Woodburn exit from Interstate 5 and continue south on Oregon 214. More creative routes can be devised on narrow, swervy country roads, but take a map.

Mt. Angel is only forty miles south of Portland, but it seems seventy-five years or so away. Gliding over two-lane roads through towns like Monitor, Aurora, and Silverton, the mood, scene, and sound change stunningly from twenty-first-century clangor to nineteenth-century rural.

Germans settled in the area in the late nineteenth century, and Bavarian-style storefronts still reflect Mt. Angel's European roots. Religion permeates the town, which is dominated by the two-hundred-foot steeple of St. Mary's Catholic Church, built in 1910 of pressed cement bricks in the Gothic Revival style. All of this is a prelude to Mount Angel Abbey, which crowns a three-hundred-foot butte on the edge of town and gazes down on a green valley where corn, hops, grass seed, Christmas trees, berries, and pumpkins are grown.

17

Swiss Benedictine monks founded the monastery in the 1880s. About fifty monks live there now and conduct a seminary and a retreat house. Rev. Michael Mee greets visitors in the retreat house. It is not a motel, he makes plain, but travelers have special standing here. Under the Benedictine rule, guests are to be received as Christ, and Catholics and non-Catholics are encouraged to stay, not only for organized retreats but for solitary days of quiet and reflection—a broad definition.

The spare guest rooms with bath are available for about sixty dollars a night, which includes meals. Father Mee may suggest in a way that is both offhand and pointed that a few days of reflection at the abbey would not preclude a visit to Silver Creek Falls nearby or a drive in the countryside. But mostly, the monastery is a place for a voyager, on the road or in life, to recover bearings and become centered after days or years of imbalance.

The quiet at Mount Angel Abbey is a white hush until the clangor of bells summons monks to mass and to prayers during the day: vigils, lauds, vespers, and compline. When the bells cease, the silence becomes a noise in itself, persistent and noticeable.

Buildings surrounding a grassy quadrangle include the abbey church, the guest house, and residence halls for students. Slid in so subtly that it can almost pass unnoticed is the abbey library, designed by Finnish architect Alvar Aalto and completed in 1970. Inside, the street voice of normal conversation resounds like a shattering dinner plate. A librarian cautions offenders to hush.

Aalto rejected architectural bravura in his design and even declined to take full advantage of the site's sweeping views. The building's purpose is study and thought, and the architect sublimated every sight and sound to those purposes. Natural light illuminates the library's muted black, white, and natural-wood palette. Aalto believed books should be the library's focus and that their bindings would provide sufficient color.

Bells sound and monks file into the silent abbey church. An organ pronounces a note, and Gregorian chant begins. The monks sing the human experience of millennia confined in a few notes. They will sing all one hundred fifty psalms every two weeks. Ask for assistance in following the chant in books provided in the abbey church vestibule. The experience of the chant is more profound if words are understood.

Cruising the velvety green Willamette Valley farm country is as calming and spiritual in its way as strolling the monastery quadrangle. Old Believers, properly known as Russian Old Orthodox, came to the Willamette Valley in the 1960s, about eighty years after the Benedictines arrived. Their community near Gervais on Bethlehem Drive remains an island of onion-domed Russian culture.

In another direction, in the town of Scotts Mills, a little Quaker church sits on a hill. And for a moving reminder of the direction that we are all heading, turn left on Oregon 213 on the way back to Mt. Angel and discover Miller Cemetery Church. Built in 1882, it was known as a burying church to generations of bereaved. The church floor slopes to the front of the building where a raised platform held the coffin for unobstructed viewing. It is as spare and functional in its way as the Mount Angel Abbey library. The focus reminds us of the big events in life, and so does the abbey's silence.

The Basics: For those who choose not to stay at the abbey, bed-and-breakfasts and a motel are available in nearby Silverton.

Dallas
15,100

The Road: Dallas can be reached quickly from Salem, traveling west on Oregon 22, but a more scenic route from north or south is Oregon 99W, which passes through the deep green Willamette Valley countryside and through towns like Rickreall, Amity, and Monroe.

Dallas, Oregon, in no particular order offers a lovely park, a downtown square that appears idyllic, at least from a distance, and a pervasive sense of history. Sewn into the green fabric of the Willamette Valley seventeen miles west of Salem, it's an overlooked jewel.

The town has a center, but coming from Salem on the buzzing Oregon 22, you wouldn't know it. The road to the downtown from the highway requires a tedious journey past a Wal-Mart, fast-food stops, gas stations, and supermarkets. But then the town center opens up, steeped in tradition, comfortably proportioned, ideal for shopping and strolling. The 1898 Polk County Courthouse announced by its forty-foot clock tower rises in the center from a square of green lawn. Surrounding on three sides are businesses housed in century-old two-story brick buildings, their facades kept mostly intact. Never mind that some storefronts are empty or house businesses that seem improvised.

White settlers arrived in the area in the 1840s and settled on La Creole Creek—later Rickreall Creek. Dallas became a prosperous center for trading and manufacture, as well as the home of La Creole Academy. The town gained notoriety in 1884 for the lynching of a man who had shot his wife in a drunken rage. A mob seized him from the jail and hung from

20

an oak tree—later called the Hanging Tree—which stood for close to a century longer until it was cut down to make room for a parking lot. The growth of the state capital of Salem, seventeen miles east, eclipsed Dallas and today it is a bedroom community, although one with character and identity and an obvious sense of civic pride. An example of the latter is the thirty-three-acre Dallas City Park, where an entire day could be spent strolling, picnicking, enjoying the Japanese Garden and the arboretum that displays native trees, shrubs, and wild flowers.

One person who is vibrantly aware of Dallas's possibilities is Penny Cox. She is tall and blond. I saw her first on a rainy night, dressed in black, singing *To Keep My Love Alive* in a barnlike structure outside Dallas that used to be a dance hall for hops pickers. In the Rodgers and Hart song, a lady from the court of King Arthur muses over the husbands she has murdered one by one. Cox nailed it.

She also performs with her own Moonfall Theater near Dallas, buys and renovates downtown buildings, and writes legal briefs on land-use issues. Her building project when I met her was renovating an old J.C. Penney store for use as an event center. This was a couple of years ago. Since then, the Dallas Event Center has opened in a splash of music and color on what had been a dark spot on a dark street. Penny and her troupe performed, and it was as glamorous an event as Dallas had seen in a while.

Penny's most recent project is conversion of a dark, worn bar across the street from the courthouse into a sophisticated restaurant, L'Attitude Point One. For this, she chose a partner, Janette Sinclair, a former executive chef of the Scottsdale Culinary Institute in Scottsdale, Arizona. She serves locally produced meat and grows vegetables for the restaurant in the yard of her home. They hope to cater to, among others, the

21

mountain bikers who throng to nearby Falls City to ride the trails on Black Rock Mountain.

Not far from the restaurant is the former headquarters of the Muir & McDonald Co. tannery, sadly closed in 2007. At the time of its demise, it was the oldest operating business in Polk County and the oldest of three tanneries in the United States using an all-vegetable tanning process. What's left is a big red hulk of a place built by volunteers in 1903 that looks like it will tumble down at any moment, which is part of its charm.

The past matters around here. A few miles outside town on Pacific Highway is the Polk County Museum, a serious institution that includes a fine display of items from the county's beginnings as well as a modest exhibit commemorating the 1950s pop star Johnnie Ray, who was raised in Dallas and vicinity. Johnnie Ray was a character. His voice even as young man had a smoky, whiskey quality, powerful and grainy. He got emotional onstage and broke down singing "Cry," or "The Little White Cloud That Cried." For a while, he was one of the biggest names out there, but his career slid in the late 1950s with the arrival of Elvis and other rockers who traded more on sex than sentiment. He died of liver failure in 1990, a few months after his last concert, which was held in Salem. It's possible to think of him hanging out in downtown Dallas, humming the tunes that were sizzling inside him.

There's no Johnnie Ray singing in Dallas today, but it's got plenty of music and dance, much of it streaming from a little white building, the Guthrie Community Center, a few miles outside town on Oregon 223. Friday nights, musicians from Dallas and surrounding towns gather in a circle for acoustic jam sessions, playing mostly swing, country, gospel, and bluegrass on violin, guitar, banjo, ukulele, bass, and anything else that's acoustic. On a typical night, you might hear "Redwing," "Blue Ridge Mt. Blues," "Down by the Riverside," and whatever else pops into the players' minds. There's also a gospel jam once a month and a monthly country square dance that's popular with young people. All of this is held in a place that started as a small rural school in 1885, although the current building probably dates from the 1920s.

It is a place that has its roots in the past, but maintains an engaging spirit that pulls in enthusiastic crowd of all ages. The spirit of Dallas is somewhat the same.

The Basics: The Riverside Inn is a clean, basic motel. The Best Western Dallas Inn is considerably more upscale.

Scio
760
Stayton
7,800
Sublimity
2,300

The Road: The best way to enjoy this pocket of the Willamette Valley is to travel the rural roads east of Interstate 5, but take along a map. Coming from the south on Interstate 5, the best exit point is Oregon 228, which passes through Brownsville. From the north, take Oregon 22.

Scio, Stayton, and Sublimity dangle like little gems strung close together in the Willamette Valley. White settlers arrived in the 1840s. Later, towns were platted and evolved into farming and industrial communities and finally as bedrooms for the nearby state capital of Salem. None of them have sunk into the torpor that can overtake a small town when its industry pulls out and residents work elsewhere. Well past the century mark, they still bear themselves confidently.

Probably the best way to appreciate them is to begin by cruising the surrounding countryside by car or bike. This is deep farm country with lanes little changed from a century ago. At Mt. Pleasant Community Church, housed in a little white wooden box built in 1854, the congregation sings "Are You Washed in the Blood of the Lamb?" with timeless energy.

In these places, be prepared to poke along at five miles an hour behind a piece of farm machinery, knowing that it may take a while to get to an intersection. The scene is green and transcendentally peaceful: gently undulating fields, stands of oak and cottonwood, farmhouses meticulously maintained by owners whose attitude toward Mother Nature allows no nonsense. Weathered barns appear everywhere and when they sag and bend, vines curl around and bear them to the ground.

Sublimity, named for its sublime scenery, is one of the oldest towns in Oregon. Its post office was founded in 1852 and St. Boniface Church, with its bold steeple, was built in 1889. The town even had a college then. Its first president was Milton Wright, father of Orville and Wilbur. For outsiders, it's mostly a drive-through place, although many stop for a tavern meal at the Wooden Nickel Pub.

Stayton, two miles down the road, began as a sawmill in 1870. Waterpower built the town and much of the water infrastructure survives today. On the edge of the Third Avenue business district is a waterway, something between a canal and a ditch, which diverted water from the Santiam River to power a local industrial complex of twelve businesses. The old downtown on Third Avenue has been supplanted by the sprawling commercial strip along First Avenue, but it still hangs on. The Star Cinema shows first-run movies and Rumours Lounge fills up on weekend nights for chat and karaoke.

Scio, a fraction the size of Stayton, lies eight miles farther on a curving road. It was incorporated in 1866, making it the tenth-oldest town in the state. Its flavor owes to three distinct waves of migration. Pioneer settlers arrived first, followed in the late 1890s by Czechoslovakians, who brought ethnic dance and food to the pioneer village. In 1957, Mennonites arrived. They took a more austere view of life than the Czechs, but their hard work and generosity in helping the town rebuild after the disastrous 1996 flood was widely respected.

The buildings on Scio's Main Street look as though they were nailed up in a couple of days with no attempt at grace or ornamentation. Still, the street harbors several distinctive businesses, including the Scio Feed and Country Store, which

25

has become an Oregon legend for Big Red, a Rhode Island rooster that used to amble freely in the downtown cadging handouts until a dog got him. After the bird's demise in 2006, the owners had him mounted and put on display in the store. Big Red has inspired a variety of products, including a polyresin Big Red figurine, available for $28.95.

Nearby on Thomas Creek stands a barnlike white structure, the ZCBJ hall. The initials stand for Zapandi Czechoslovakia Brakaska Jednota, or Western Czechoslovakian Fraternal Association. The Czechs used it for community gatherings and although the Linn County Lamb & Wool Fair owns it now, it's still a place where good times roll.

Friday nights, it looks like a landmine could explode in downtown Scio and no one would bother to report it, but the action is all indoors. For an evening of entertainment, make it the last Friday of the month. Start at the Olde Silver Dollar, which looks dark and solemn from the street, but is jumping inside. Friday night prime rib is reported to be the best in the area. At 7:30 p.m., musicians converge on the ZCBJ hall just down the street for a bluegrass jam. They saw, strum, and plunk on mandolin, fiddle, bass, and guitar. The music is loose and improvised, and the jams can last until early morning. On one occasion, a ten-year-old boy threw back his head and delivered in a marvelously twangy voice an old bluegrass song, "Don't Sell Daddy Anymore Whiskey" while daddy fiddled. The transition from the Olde Silver Dollar to the ZCBJ Hall was seamless.

26

The Basics: The Rodeway Inn on a hill between Stayton and Sublimity is comfortable and modern. The Wooden Nickel in Sublimity and the Olde Silver Dollar in Scio are known for good food served in a pub atmosphere. The Lovin' Oven in Stayton is popular for lunch.

Brownsville
1,755

The Road: The quickest way to get to Brownsville coming from the north is to take Interstate 5 and leave the freeway south of Albany at Oregon 228 east. Coming from the south, an alternate route is to leave the freeway on Oregon 126 at Springfield, turn left at the Mohawk Boulevard exit and right onto Marcola Road, get off at 19th Street and follow Marcola Road north to Crawfordsville and continue west on Oregon 228.

Brownsville lies a few miles off Interstate 5, far enough to prevent it from becoming a freeway stop and close enough to keep it spry when many towns its age and size are creaky. To reach the downtown, cross the Calapooia River and pass a big white church on the left. Continue past a handsome Italianate structure, the Moyer House, now a museum, and enter the downtown, which is the very model of a quaint business district from about a century ago.

A thin overlay of tourism—some cute lettering and a gingerbready porch dreamed up in the 1960s—make Brownsville seem more touristy than it is. In fact, it is a real town where people know each other and participate energetically in the town's many annual events, including a croquet tournament and the Linn County Pioneer Picnic. Nights, people drop in to the Brownsville Saloon or the Corner Cafe. The town has no movie theater, but the Linn County Historical Museum shows old films regularly in its twenty-six-seat theater.

People talk proudly of their town's history and often of their family's place in the scheme of it. Old families still live quietly in town and on farms that are pushed into the fabric

27

of the valley like buttons on green plush. Among them are the Drinkards, whose forebears came to Oregon in a covered wagon in 1865. The wagon, one of only a handful of pioneer trail wagons that still exist, is displayed in the Linn County Historical Museum.

Atavista Farm, a setting for weddings and special events housed in an 1876 Italianate house outside town, is heavy with a sense of history and the lives that were led there. To sit in the parlor and look out a high window to the fields is to feel life as it was a hundred and fifty years earlier. The experience can be as gray as the dripping clouds outside. Owner Sharon McCoy allows curious visitors to examine a small, worn volume, the diary of Amelia Spalding Brown, who lived there in the 1870s and '80s. She was an invalid who had lost two children as infants, and the diary records an anguished life. She must have known the view from the parlor well.

The best times in a small town often come from hanging out: browsing in downtown stores, chatting with the town historian, having an early cup of coffee in a local café. At Randy's Main Street Coffee, owner Randy Ginn is at work by 4:30 a.m. baking bread, rolls, and egg bake (a filling dish of eggs and cheese and hashbrowns). By about 7 a.m., the Geezers are drifting in to the little café that smells of coffee and hot fresh bread and pulling up chairs at what has come to be known as the Geezers' Table. The Geezers are mostly men and often include retirees, firemen, a writer on local history, and the mayor, who is also publisher of the newspaper. They laugh and banter, consuming oceans of coffee while explaining the world according to Brownsville.

In the winter as dark gray skies pour water on Main Street, the place seems even more a refuge and talk flows freely. You can learn about life in a place like this, and if not about life, at least about the places to go and things to see in Brownsville. These might include a couple of wonderful oddities that capture the history and spirit of the place. One is a rock shop. The other is a log cabin, hidden in plain sight.

From the road, the concrete and stone Living Rock Studios is a goblin's castle, brooding and fanciful. Inside, Nancy Bergerson welcomes guests with the attitude of a keeper of the flame. The flame is the spirit of her father, Howard Taylor, who came to Brownsville in 1952 and worked as a surveyor. In his spare time, he collected rocks. Illness forced his retirement in 1964 and passion became a fulltime job. He amassed eight hundred tons of rock for the structure's building blocks: lava, agates, petrified wood, jasper, quartz, obsidian, and sandstone. A gallery showcases scenes from the Bible composed in thin slices of translucent rock. A stairwell in the shape of a tree trunk rises from the center. On the second floor, the trunk puts out great stone branches set with rare and curious rocks.

Not far from the rock studios just off Oregon 228 stands a twenty-six-foot-high structure supported by Douglas fir columns. A rustic-style wood porch extends its length and a wide door opens to the interior. Inside this structure with plenty of room on all sides stands a twenty-by-thirty-foot log cabin, built of hand-hewn Douglas fir slabs. It's held together at the corners by dovetail joints—miraculous carpentry considering the weight of the logs and the tools that were available to work them.

Greg Hopla, a big, ruddy fellow with long black hair that he ties in a ponytail, owns the place, which was passed down through generations of his family. The cabin was built as a trading post by Alexander Kirk, one of the first whites to settle in the vicinity. Kirk established a ferry across the Calapooia River, and for a time the community was known as Kirk's

29

Ferry. Later the name was changed to Brownsville in honor of a local merchant.

Like most ancient log cabins in Oregon, the age of this one is unclear. Hopla says his grandmother said it was built in 1846 and urged him not to accept a later date. If the 1846 date is correct, it certainly would be among the oldest standing log cabins in Oregon. (The Baker cabin, which is not far from Estacada, is also considered one of the oldest, but it was built a decade later in 1856.)

For almost a century, the cabin sat hidden in another skin. Probably in the early twentieth century, the cabin's owners decided to build a modern house on the site, but instead of tearing down the log cabin, they incorporated it into their home, attaching siding to the squared-off Douglas fir logs. Over the years, the house in its nailed-on housecoat began to look feeble and decrepit with little sign of the noble old structure it concealed. Hopla, however, sizzles and pops with plans for the place. An entrepreneur with a fanciful streak, he runs a small business manufacturing titanium swords, battle axes, and wooden souvenir swords. As a young man, he worked for Renaissance Faires in California and later for Medieval Times, which builds castles around the country and stages medieval-style jousts and battles using Hopla's weaponry.

Over a few years, he built a steel and log canopy to protect the house. Then he ripped away the cabin's siding and built the surrounding structure. He wants the cabin to be the centerpiece of an educational and period performance center. He also has plans for dinner theater with shows that will dramatize the area's history.

It's a haunting symbol of the past now, buried in Brownsville's present.

The Basics: Atavista Farm, once the largest bed-and-breakfast in town, no longer takes guests. There's another B & B, The Nest, which offers a small cottage close to the downtown. Four miles west of town on Oregon 228 at Interstate 5 is a Travelodge motel. There are several spots for meals in the downtown, including Randy's Main Street Coffee and the Corner Cafe.

31

Harrisburg

3,400

The Road: Harrisburg is twenty-four miles from Eugene and most easily reached from Interstate 5, taking exit 209 and traveling west. Coming from the north, a more scenic route is Oregon 99W, which passes through the heart of Willamette Valley farm country.

Harrisburg has occupied its bend of the Willamette River since 1852, which is, for Oregon, a long time to sit in one place. The river makes a lazy curve here, running beneath a bridge and along the edge of town. From a distance, it looks glassy and slow, but summer swimmers beware—the current is forceful and it takes strong, fast strokes to stay where you are. Succulent fields of ryegrass stretch in all directions, and for a calming interlude, take a bike or car trip into this pastoral landscape, dotted with groves of trees and classic farm houses. The town itself doesn't live up to its surroundings. Much of it looks drab and neglected, especially the downtown, where the deterioration is made all the more poignant by the many elderly brick buildings that patiently await the town's renaissance.

The big news from Harrisburg is the River Bend Resort, which opened in spring 2009, giving the town overnight lodging and the potential to attract free-spending tourists with its ninety-five RV spaces, nineteen hotel rooms, and banquet facilities. It is just a mile or so outside Harrisburg, and town leaders and businesspeople hope that this nice little resort will create demand for new businesses in the downtown. The developers of River Bend, however, couldn't have chosen a worse time to open their doors. The resort was built to take advantage of high-roller RV owners who purchased their

32

vehicles from Monaco Coach, manufacturer of recreational vehicles, and brought them to the Monaco service center in Harrisburg for maintenance. The recession and high fuel prices sent Monaco into bankruptcy, but it has been purchased by another company.

Culturally and geographically, Harrisburg is a river town. That's its past and probably its future as well. It got a big break in December 1862, when a flood inundated the valley and washed away houses and livestock. When the water receded, the river's course had changed, leaving the competing town of Lancaster no longer on the river. As a result, river commerce shifted to Harrisburg and farmers brought their crops there for shipment.

Today, the river is used less for commerce and more for recreation. A fanciful white gazebo commands Riverfront Park, and in the summer, local businesses sponsor concerts and movies there. Until recently, anyone who wanted to get on the river had to bring their own boat, but that changed when hardware store owner Mike Hurd and partner Tadge Cook bought a wrecked jet boat, fixed it up, and offered two- and three-hour trips. Oregon rivers come in sizes and speeds from roaring and reckless to slow and serene. The Willamette in this stretch belongs in the latter category, although winter storms and runoff can push the water up several feet and propel clots of dangerous logs careening downstream. At all times, it is tree-lined and intriguing, snaking through some of the state's most fertile farmland and teeming with water birds and four-footed critters.

Even those who prefer to stay close to the water should stop by the Harrisburg Area Museum. Small-town museums can tend toward sameness, because over generations, we all lead the same lives with the same needs and the same tools. The Harrisburg museum stands out because it's spacious, with

33

several buildings exhibiting big things, like a thresher, trucks, and steam tractors, as well as some smaller things you won't see anywhere else.

Bruce Witmer was a master carpenter who came to Harrisburg in 1959 from Pennsylvania and built miniature structures as a hobby. A room at the museum displays fifty-one of his pieces, all exquisitely detailed. His miniature Noah's Ark is sized to biblical specifications at a quarter-inch to the foot, and includes three hundred animal pens, eighteen water tanks, and eighty-four sliding windows. He also built a model of Crater Lake Lodge and replicas of local buildings.

And even if Harrisburg's downtown is a forlorn example of a great place waiting to be put to good use, there remain several businesses with plenty of life in them. Among them is Barter Bill's (sometimes it's referred to as Trader Bill's), a secondhand and antiques store on Second Street. It is the vision of Bill Terrell and he himself calls it "a wonderful mess," which indeed it is. He has collected glassware, pottery, fine china, textiles, art, books, jewelry, tools, records, furniture—the mind reels. Customers drop in from all over the world, alerted to the place by word of mouth, since he doesn't advertise. Some of his most intriguing items won't meet any test of good taste, such as the pair of ceramic candlesticks, fashioned as bony, ill-manicured hands, flexed like tarantulas.

"I also like the unusual," he says. "Some things that are so unusual that I don't know what they are."

I can think of only two other secondhand shops in Oregon that can hold a candle to this place: Mike's Second Hand Store in Estacada, and Old Stuff in Cottage Grove, both noted in this book.

And for a snack or an early dinner after a visit to Barter Bill's, walk across the street to Air Thai Cuisine, housed in

34

a square brick building painted a curious shade of green. Proprietor and chef Khambang Air Chanthabandith offers about eighty dishes including curries, salads, soups, sautés, and noodles. Chinese restaurants for decades have been fixtures in small Northwest towns, opening a wide world to people who otherwise stayed close to home. Lately, Thai restaurants also are moving in, adding another ethnicity and another exotic cuisine. It may be a good sign for Harrisburg's future that it is riding the trend.

The Basics: Air Thai Cuisine is a fine place for dinner or lunch. Outfitters Bar and Grill on Smith Street downtown serves steaks, burgers, and pasta. A popular breakfast spot is Jake's Café on Third Street.

35

Cottage Grove
9,300

The Road: Cottage Grove straddles Interstate 5, which means that a freeway trip is inevitable coming from north or south.

A forest of signs peddling gas, beds, and road food announces Cottage Grove from Interstate 5. Beyond the gas-stop clutter is a fine old main street, a romantic river that glides through town, and an offbeat sensibility that may be its future.

The town's gently lulling atmosphere encourages drift. Main Street is a step back into another century, or would be if it were busier. Shops that would bring customers here on a daily basis are long gone, replaced by book and antiques shops, some restaurants, and a couple of bars. On warm afternoons, Stacy's Covered Bridge places tables on the sidewalk for a relaxing lunch on the quiet street. Afterward, you can stroll on River Road along the Coast Fork of the Willamette River.

You will pass the Old Mill Farm Store, which dates from 1853, when it was a grist mill. In 1906, the water wheel supplied the town's first electricity to six street lights. Traces of the old structure remain, and an adjacent barn, probably built in the late nineteenth century, sags like a drunken miller. Beyond the farm store, a suspension footbridge hangs above the Coast Fork of the Willamette River. In the other direction, near the downtown, the Cottage Grove Museum at Birch and H streets displays an intriguing collection of old stuff, including a heavy woolen coat that warmed a local woman, Marion Wright, on a lifeboat when the Titanic sank. There's also a wreath composed of human hair, a scale model of a water-powered sawmill, a 1912 lawnmower, a variety of hand-powered washing machines, and a table for laying out a corpse.

The first white settlers arrived in the area in 1847. A general store was erected ten years later and gold was discovered in the mountains the next year. The classic downtown and the lovely natural surroundings attracted filmmakers over the years, the most important of them Buster Keaton, who filmed his 1926 Civil War adventure, *The General,* in the country around Cottage Grove. Today, a wall painting of the comedian, stone faced and handsome, looms at one end of Main Street. The Cottage Grove Historical Society still celebrates Buster Keaton Day on the third Saturday of October. The town prospered until the decline of the forest-products industry changed all that. Still, it teems with possibilities. The twentieth century left Cottage Grove in the lurch; the twenty-first may pick it up again.

Brad van Appel believes he saw the future when he and two others bought and gutted a 1908 downtown mercantile building. They peeled away layers of carpet, tile, and paneling to reveal the original light-flooded structure. Now, a barber, a bookstore, a bakery, and a pub, the Axe and Fiddle, occupy the airy space. On a weekend night, the Axe and Fiddle is a golden lantern on the dark street. Inside, people huddle at tables and the bar for blues, bluegrass, and jazz. In the morning, presumably some of the same people read, eat scones, and answer e-mail in the space.

Whether the renovation marks the beginning of a downtown renaissance or a bump on a downhill slide isn't certain. I have a hunch that Cottage Grove's future may lie outside the mainstream. Consider Old Stuff, a secondhand store on the edge of town on Highway 99 South. Al Neuenfeldt owns it. He ties a hippie-style bandana on his head and calls his business "a twenty-three-year yard sale." He trades in "anything that looks cool." In stock on one day were neon beer signs, record albums and rock posters from the 1960s, bold and curious paintings, musical instruments, bizarre crockery, old machines and appliances, and a tie-dyed American flag.

Outside town, roads and lanes lead to breathtaking views. From Fairview Peak, reached by a dizzying drive up dirt roads, Mt. Shasta can be seen to the south and Mt. Hood to the north. And for walking or biking, the Row River Trail begins in the downtown historic district and continues fifteen miles on a paved track, past farms, forest, and Dorena Lake.

It would be nice to see Cottage Grove grow, renovate, and become a distinctive presence among Oregon I-5 towns. On the other hand, it is pretty nice as it is.

The Basics: The best place to stay in Cottage Grove is the Village Green Resort, a well-known Oregon lodging that has made a comeback recently under new owners after a long decline. Stacy's Covered Bridge is a popular restaurant and has a good downtown location. The Backstage Bakery in the Burkholder-Woods building (home of the Axe and Fiddle) is a pleasant stop for breakfast. Information about points of interest, roads, and trails in the vicinity is available at the U.S. Forest Service office on Cedar Park Road.

38

Oakridge
3,680

The Road: From Eugene to Oakridge on Oregon 58, the road climbs past silvery-green lakes and hills swathed in pelts of Douglas fir. This is the Willamette National Forest, the heart of Oregon timber country.

Oakridge from the highway is a dowdy, two-mile commercial strip: a couple of restaurants, some motels, a supermarket, and a gas station. It takes conscious effort to look above the roofline and discover that, in every direction, hills rise in densely forested banks.

Its setting in the Willamette National Forest is one of the most stunningly beautiful in Oregon, and along with its sister city of Westfir (population 276), it is the only city in Oregon completely surrounded by national forest. In the vicinity are Salt Creek Falls, the state's second-highest waterfall, the West Cascade National Scenic Byway, at least twenty-four campgrounds, an extensive network of nature trails, and a ski area. The Middle Fork of the Willamette River flows past Oakridge, beginning as a small outlet of Waldo Lake east of Oakridge, then dropping twenty-four hundred feet in three miles and plunging over thirty-four separate waterfalls. On the edge of Oakridge at Greenwaters Park, a visitor can sit on rocks at the river's edge and enjoy its tumultuous passage. A bridge spans the river and leads to a trail that extends deep into the forest.

At the Willamette Fish Hatchery just outside town, there's a one-thousand-year-old slab of Douglas fir incised with a map that shows the tracery of creeks and rivers that begin high in the Cascades and feed the Willamette River. The water rushing

39

down the mountains and millions of trees pumping moisture create a singular ecosystem. Andrea Hodges, a newcomer to town, lives in a house on a hill that commands magnificent views of the town and the mountains. "You can see the mountains steaming and popping off little clouds," she says. "It's like living in a cloud machine."

There are not many views of Oakridge from above. The best is near the thirty-four-foot white cross that towers on a hill above the city, but it's on private property. The owner says he built it as a reminder to the people of Oakridge of God's love for them. It's possible to get a lesser view on some public property nearby. You can find it by taking Airport Road west of town and following it past the airport.

White settlers began pushing into the vicinity of Oakridge in the 1850s. The arrival of the railroad in 1912 meant that timber could be exported from here, and for years Oakridge and nearby Westfir boomed as trees were cut, processed, and sent off to build America. But the last sawmill closed in the early 1990s and Oakridge sat stranded in the woods, forty miles from Eugene and Interstate 5. At its height, Oakridge had ten bars, a measure, one might say, of disposable income. It has two at last count, and most of the family-wage jobs are with the Oakridge School District and the U.S. Forest Service.

In the Oakridge Museum on Pine Street in the old town, the tumult and ambition of the past with all its odd, ingenious machinery and weighty lugs of metal and wood is on view. Among the artifacts are chainsaws, an ancient wooden yoke for carrying buckets of water, the remains of a wagon dating to the 1850s found in the mountains by loggers, and a wooden water wheel from a gold mine.

But the future of Oakridge may have less to do with lifting heavy things than with pushing and pumping. If timber executives don't see a future in the mountains, bikers certainly do. Within a thirty-mile radius of Oakridge are three hundred and fifty miles of bike trails that snake up and down the hillsides, cross creeks, and come to the crest of mountains that command heart-stopping views.

The reinvention of Oakridge as an eco-tourism capital can't be far away. One sign could be Brewers Union Local 180, a brewpub that replaced a rundown tavern on First Street, which was once the main business street but feels empty now. That too may change.

Ted Sobel, the owner of the pub, came to Oakridge in 1991 from upstate New York. An enthusiastic Anglophile, he spent vacations trekking Great Britain, enjoying its atmospheric pubs along the way. It occurred to him that bikers, just like trekkers, would like a convivial place to end the day, drink a couple of pints, and eat some tasty bar food. He and a partner gutted and renovated the old tavern and gave it a new and eccentric name. Loosely modeled on the Woolpack Inn in the English Lake District, it serves real ale, which is unfiltered and unpasteurized and served warmer than American beers.

Locals wished him well, but some wondered if old-timers or newcomers would settle for room-temperature brew when they could have an ice cold fizzy Bud. But people seem to enjoy this congenial spot, built with conviction and an eye for what active, venturesome people like.

41

The Basics: The first stop approaching Oakridge from the west on Route 58 should be the Willamette National Forest's Middle Fork Ranger Station, which provides reams of helpful information about area attractions. The Cascade Motel in Oakridge offers clean, inexpensive rooms and helpful management. There are several restaurants in town, including Chinese and Mexican.

Oregon Coast

Oregon Coast

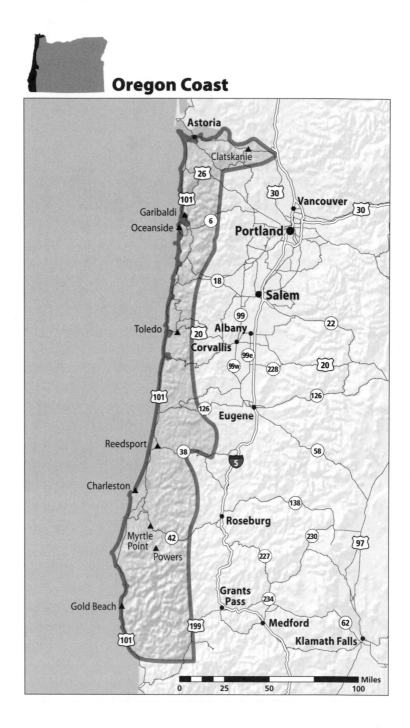

Clatskanie
1,700

The Road: The road to Clatskanie from Portland on U.S. 30 passes along the final stretch of the Columbia River where the Lewis and Clark Expedition neared the end of their cross-continent journey. On the way, the town of Rainier is worth a stop for its waterfront and views of the industrial plants of Longview across the river. The view of glittering lights and smoking machinery is at its grandest from a highway turnout on a hill just north of Rainier.

Clatskanie from the road reveals little of the town's character. Its main street is a continuation of Oregon 30, and motorists usually speed through on the way to Astoria and the Oregon coast. Roadside businesses look disheveled, and other than the highway strip, there appears to be no center to the place. The real Clatskanie and the real business district have to be searched out. Appearances here can't be trusted. Consider Humps.

From the west, it looks like a bikers' bar and the name suggests something even rougher. It is actually a restaurant, and gets its name from Forris Humphrey, who opened it in 1948. Since then, it has been remodeled and rebuilt several times, most recently after a 1989 fire. Inside, it is airy and tranquil with an attitude of gracious gentility.

After lunch at Humps, take a left and walk down Nehalem Street, which is the town's true business district and almost invisible from the highway. It's cozy and comfortable and offers most things a person needs to carry on life—post office, grocery, hardware, bank, and a couple of bars. Phil Hazen owns the hardware store and his wife, Deborah Steele Hazen, works next door at *The Clatskanie Chief*, the local newspaper.

Her grandfather bought the paper in 1922 and she's the third generation of Steeles to run it. A steady stream of kibitzers stop by to pass the time of day or drop a juicy bit. She knows everyone's story or how to find it out, and the newspaper she puts out is crammed to the masthead with news and information.

Only two miles from the Columbia River, the town is steeped in river lore. The Lewis and Clark Expedition passed by in 1805 and 1806 and William Clark named an island a few miles northeast of Clatskanie for his sister Fanny. (It is now known as Crims Island.) White settlers moved to the area in the 1870s, and the town got its name from the Tlatskanai Indians who lived in the hills south of the Clatskanie River. For years, a steamboat was the only way in and out of town.

To get a feel for this part of the country, rise early, take a thermos of coffee, and drive west toward Astoria. On a winter day, fog off the marshy fields meets low gray clouds and, if it's raining, the sky and the fields seem one. In the early 1900s, farmers drained the flat lowland along the river and built dikes and drainage canals, creating farmland where they grew mint and grass seed. In the 1940s, Columbia County was the largest producer of mint oil in the United States. You hear Clatskanie and vicinity called Little Holland, but that's mostly a reference to the dikes. There are few if any Dutch in these parts but lots of Finns and Swedes.

A few miles from Clatskanie at Weston, the Wahkiakum Ferry, the last ferry on the lower Columbia, can carry nine cars across the river to Puget Island. This is only a ten-minute voyage, but it's stirring and romantic, especially in the winter as the vessel rumbles across the water in the fog.

Even if Little Holland is more aptly called Little Sweden or Little Finland, there is at least one reminder of the land of tulips and windmills. Outside Humps's dining-room window, there's an overgrown patch of green from which rises a little

46

blue and white windmill. The builder of this mechanism is John Lillich, who owns a mini storage and several other businesses. When John was eleven, his parents took him to Holland, where the windmills fascinated him. He later built his own wind machines at 20 to 40 percent scale. He sold a couple of the structures but several are up and running on the property. Lillich says they can perform small tasks like sharpening knives and generating minor amounts of electricity.

Nehalem Street continues out of town into the wet green countryside. Signs direct to Great Vow Zen Monastery on Quincy-Mayger Road, which occupies a former elementary school built in 1971 and later abandoned. When the Zen priests (they call them priests rather than monks to avoid gender stamping) found it, spiders and mold had invaded, but the structure seemed providentially designed for their purposes, with glassed-in interior gardens, long contemplative halls, and serene, spacious rooms.

Great Vow's intent is to embody qualities of optimism, fearlessness, and benevolence, states of mind that suggest encounter with a troubled world. And it's true that the image of monks as withdrawn and otherworldly is contradicted at Great Vow, where the priests are hospitable and outgoing. Fran, who has been in residence only a year, cheerfully shows visitors through the monastery. With the rest of the community, she rises before dawn and spends the day in work and four hours of contemplation. But members regularly emerge from seclusion to attend Kiwanis and teach marimba at the local elementary school. From here, Quincy-Mayger Road executes a loop through the forest that at one point opens to sweeping views of the river, and ends at U.S. 30—a route as calming as the monastery.

47

The Basics: Humps is the place to eat in Clatskanie, and the Clatskanie River Inn is a comfortable motel.

Garibaldi

900

The Road: Garibaldi is on U.S. 101, about ten miles north of
Tillamook. Taking this road allows a stop at the Tillamook
County Pioneer Museum. A more scenic route coming from
Portland is to take U.S. 26 to Necanicum Junction and then
travel south on Oregon 53, the Necanicum Highway, to U.S. 101
and continue to Garibaldi.

The road north from the town of Tillamook curves along
Tillamook Bay on one side and forested hills on the other.
Garibaldi, with its 205-foot concrete smokestack, appears
suddenly around a curve, an unexpected intrusion of
industrial architecture into a landscape of water and trees. The
smokestack is an anomaly now on the Oregon coast, where the
economy has shifted from heavy industry to recreation. It used
to disperse smoke from a lumber mill, long since bulldozed
and converted to an RV park. Even if the jobs aren't there
now, the symbolism remains.

Gentrification hasn't arrived in Garibaldi, which sets it apart
on the coast. Even little Wheeler on Nehalem Bay a few miles
north offers art galleries and a nice hotel/bed-and-breakfast.
It may be the town's location on the bay and not the ocean
that has isolated it from the surf and sun mentality of coastal
towns and also discouraged an invasion of lifestyle seekers. It's
a place that lives on water, makes its living from water, finds
its spirits lifted daily by vistas of forest, river, and bay.

Start with the bay. It's about six miles long, extending from
the mouth just north of Garibaldi almost to Tillamook. Five
rivers dump into it, the Trask, Tillamook, Wilson, Kilchis, and

48

Miami, meaning that it is flushed and refreshed by tides and rivers. Clams, crab, and oysters flourish in its waters and the rivers support steelhead and salmon runs.

Try stopping for a sunset drink at the Troller Lounge in the boat basin. The dimming light flows through west-facing windows, and conversation rises and falls in a woolly rumble. Most of the patrons aren't weekenders. They have stories to tell, maybe about fishing and crabbing, the lousy catch and the way the industry has nose-dived over the years. It's a convivial small-town atmosphere. People here know each others' parents, children, spouses, and life stories. If other coast towns seem transient, this one has its roots deep in the ground.

One reason for Garibaldi's rich texture may be the skeins of history and tragedy woven into its fabric. Capt. Robert Gray anchored here in 1788 but left in a hurry after a fracas with local Indians. On his next voyage in 1792, Gray happened on the Great River of the West, which he named for his ship, the *Columbia*. A few miles north is Neahkahnie Mountain, celebrated for its aura of myth and mystery. According to one theory, Sir Francis Drake's party came ashore there in 1579 and laid out an English township. Stones have been found on the mountain carved with mysterious lines; it has been suggested that they could be triangulation lines for a land survey. Whether or not Drake's party carved them, they are undoubtedly mysterious. At some point the stones were hauled off to the Tillamook County Pioneer Museum where they lie in a dim display case.

Tragedy is constant. Every year or so, a boat founders crossing the bar of Tillamook Bay and lives are lost—more than two hundred, it is said, since 1867. A stirring memorial to fishermen lost at sea stands in the boat basin area on Coast Guard Way. Three benches face the memorial. Beyond is the

49

bay and Kincheloe Point, near where Julius Kincheloe and five of his crew perished in 1867.

To feel the crash of bay and ocean, drive to Barview, a few miles north of Garibaldi, clamber out on the north jetty, and watch the waves as they are funneled like angry bulls through the north and south jetties. Beyond the jetty is a fine expanse of beach, and beyond that, the looming darkness of Neahkahnie Mountain.

Hard work and danger and maybe a common sense of financial fragility seem to draw Garibaldi together. By one count, nine bars within a fifteen-mile radius, including at least two in Garibaldi, offer karaoke, which makes everyone a star for a few minutes. Also, every Friday night, local musicians gather in the Community Hall for the weekly Asleep at the Switch, a democratic jam session. Players sit in a row and for two hours bring forth country, old standards, and some gospel. If singers or players sometimes hit wrong notes and waver off key, it's still authentic and engaging as musicians adjust tempo and figure out where the others are going. They adapt and carry on, characteristic, it seems, of Garibaldi.

50

The Basics: There are two, maybe three motels in town, and several restaurants where fresh fish dinners are on the menu. The Garibaldi Pub and Eatery across from the Comfort Inn is a warm, dim place to escape from a gray sky for breakfast or for a beer later in the day. A popular local dinner house is Pirates Cove just north of town. The Tillamook Estuaries Partnership on Commercial Street in the boat basin is a good source of maps and information.

Oceanside
350

The Road: The most scenic way to reach Oceanside is to begin in Tillamook and continue out on Third Street to Bayocean Road. Turn right and you will be on the Three Capes Scenic Loop, which skirts Tillamook Bay and passes Cape Meares. There, it's a short walk to the Cape Meares Lighthouse and also to the tallest Sitka Spruce in Oregon. Continue on to Oceanside.

The road into Oceanside from Cape Meares winds down a hill, and at the base, a right turn leads to Pacific Avenue and a secluded little business district that parallels the beach. This is no coastal carnival, screaming for attention. Everything here seems deliberately understated except the view. Steep, forested mountains rise behind it stacked with a collection of houses, many in a 1960s ocean-view style. On one side of the street is a motel and farther down a restaurant, Roseanna's. Across the street stands a hulking three-story building, once the beloved Anchor Tavern, that's empty and for sale at this writing. Beyond are a post office, a community center, and a little café. Light floods the street on a sunny day and most of the time it's nearly empty except for a few people strolling in to pick up mail or to line up for a meal at Roseanna's.

51

The beach is a long, wide expanse that's also nearly deserted most days. Cape Lookout appears in the distance, and immediately to the north, the rock mass of Maxwell Point creates a towering wall. Rising from the ocean a half mile from the point is the Three Arch Rocks National Wildlife Refuge, a collection of three large and six smaller rocks.

Of the Oregon beach towns, Oceanside is among the most secluded and least swamped by tourism development, probably because it's off U.S. 101 and has to be reached by zigzagging through Tillamook. Tourists still find their way here but tourist flotsam hasn't followed them; there are no T-shirt shacks, kite shops, saltwater taffy stands, brew pubs, or wine bars. The focus is on the beach, the immense rocks and arches that stand offshore, and the birds that circle above the wildlife refuge.

Life proceeds at a tranquil pace, but occasionally something happens that riles people. Consider the Anchor Tavern controversy. It had been a local institution since 1940 serving drinks and good food. Then a new owner bought it and added a third story to create hotel rooms. It seemed out of scale with the rest of the street and blocked the ocean view of houses behind it. Locals boycotted the place and neither of two owners has been able to make a go of it.

Since Oceanside has disdained most tourist amusements, it's up to visitors to amuse themselves, and the best way to do so is hang out. There's no pressure to parasail, surf, or whale watch; efforts at self improvement are pretty much limited to walking or jogging the beach.

A day can begin with breakfast in Brewin' in the Wind, a sunny little coffee shop near the beach. This could take a couple of hours if it includes eating, reading the newspaper, and checking e-mail. Then walk Pacific Avenue and observe the people on the sleepy street if any are out and around. It's likely you will come upon Jim Lawrence, sitting on a bench in front of the post office. He has the attitude of a village chronicler, and that's what he is. He's lived in Oceanside since 1993—actually in the The Capes, a cliff-top development just outside town. Once a skater with the Ice Capades, and later a business executive, he's typical of people who have found their way to Oceanside, many of them retired, often leaving long and distinguished careers. In Oceanside, they serve on boards

52

and volunteer for local projects. "Life is like walking down a hallway," Lawrence says. "Doors open."

One door that has swung open for him is creative writing. He finds his material on the bench, striking up conversations with visitors passing by. Sometimes they come to this little town on the edge of Oregon from halfway around the world.

Then there is the beach to be walked, and the Three Arch rocks to admire. President Teddy Roosevelt in 1907 declared it a national wildlife refuge, the first west of the Mississippi River. It is habitat for Oregon's largest breeding colony of Tufted Puffins and the largest breeding colony of the Common Murre south of Alaska. It is also the only pupping site on the north Oregon Coast for the Steller sea lion.

The beach ends at Maxwell Point, which could have blocked sand-strollers from continuing on to explore the beach beyond unless they could circle around the rock at low tide. But early developers of Oceanside, J. H. and H. H. Rosenberg, solved the problem in 1926 by blasting a tunnel about a half block long through the rock, giving access to Short Beach and to Lost Boy Cave Beach. A landslide closed the tunnel in 1979, although storms sluiced it open from time to time, but in 1999, a big storm flushed it out properly.

53

Another sign that life is different here is the presence of only two places that serve food: Brewin' in the Wind, and Roseanna's. Most beach towns of this size would have twenty or so. Roseanna's has become an institution on the Oregon coast, housed in a 1923 building that was once a grocery store. On the menu one night were crab cakes, scallops, steamer clams, snapper, salmon, halibut, and Willapa Bay oysters. It's an offhand kind of place, even a little rundown, like a beach house furnished with castoffs. When Roseanna's closes for the night, the street goes dark and will stay that way until light creeps back the next morning.

The Basics: The Clifftop, a motel on the top of Maxwell Point, has the best views. The Oceanside Motel on the main street is closer to the beach. Farther down the street are the more rustic Ocean Front Cabins. The only place for a drink in the vicinity is the Schooner down the road in Netarts.

Toledo
3,585

The Road: Toledo is seven miles east of Newport and can be reached from Oregon 20 or on Yaquina Bay Road.

Most travelers whip past Toledo on Oregon 20 on their way to Newport. Although close to the ocean, it is more a river than a coast place, and its commercial soul lies in manufacturing, not fishing and tourism.

You'll get a better sense of it if you approach it not from the highway but from Newport's bayfront. Continue on Bay Boulevard until it becomes Yaquina Bay Road. The thirteen-mile road should be driven slowly to savor the bay and river. It's thronged with birds, including cormorants, herons, geese, loons, and an occasional bald eagle, that come here to feed. Humans also feed on the oysters that have been grown commercially here since 1863. You can still pull over and buy fresh oysters at Oregon Oyster Farms, founded early in the century by the Wachsmuth family to supply their Portland restaurant, Dan and Louie's Oyster Bar. Nearer Toledo, the road ascends and a magnificent panorama of the town and the Georgia-Pacific pulp and paper mill spreads below.

Newport looks timid compared to this mighty expanse of pipes, logs, wood chips, tanks, towers, and a smokestack erupting billows of white smoke that turn pink, gold, and mauve in the setting sun; no condos in sight, no cunning boutiques, just a place where muscle and machine cooperate to make container board used for boxes and packaging. The mill can turn out 2,500 tons a day and it's the largest recycler of wastepaper in Oregon. About five hundred people work

55

here, four hundred of them hourly and the rest salaried. On the coast, where the forest products industry has dwindled to a fraction of what it once was, this booming plant gives the town a vitality lacking in many small towns that have lost their core industry.

In his workshop in full view of the mill, sculptor Sam Briseno hammers out a product of a different kind. He collects big rusty pieces of scrap metal, much of it from ships, and creates assemblages that may turn up in parks, yards, and living rooms. Sometimes he makes representational pieces— steel herons or trees—but he would rather allow his work to evolve from instinct and happenstance into something more suggestive than a photo image. He isn't the only artist to move to town and take advantage of its lower real estate costs, the climate—which is said to be warmer and clearer than Newport's—and also its promise of opportunity. Several artists have established studios and galleries in the town's arts district on Alder Street. Art may never replace container board as the economic heart of this town, but it lends gloss and buzz.

Toledo's Main Street business district is one of the few on the coast that doesn't straddle a highway, which gives it an intimacy and proportion that a highway strip can't match. There are too many empty storefronts and ragtag businesses, but the basics of a downtown are there: the city hall, several bars, a Mexican restaurant, a nice regional museum, and the two-story Yaquina Bay Hotel.

Plans are underway to refurbish the street and spruce up building facades. Already the hotel has undergone a makeover under its new owner, a former Korean high-tech executive, Kook-Jin Lim. Lim was bouncing back and forth between the United States and Korea when he decided to switch from semiconductors to a small-town hotel. He has polished, painted, and updated its thirty-two rooms and he hopes to attract customers drawn by the art galleries, town festivals, and music events that proliferate in Toledo.

Frank Jones spans the new and the old Toledo. He's not there as much as he used to be, but you still can hear him sing and play guitar if he's in town. Jones sings with the gritty voice of experience. He rode the rails as a young man and moved to Toledo in 1974. Then drink caught up with him, and he moved to Portland and played the streets. He came back to Toledo in 1991, newly sober, and became a driver in the music scene—he's been called the cultural mayor of Toledo. Until recently, he stuck close to home, but then the road and the rails called. He's been spending much of his time touring the country by Amtrak. He'll go to the observation car, pull out his guitar and start singing. He looks for songs with a story—beginning, middle, and end—and he likes to sing about people "who fall between the cracks." He knows hundreds of songs and he can play for hours without repeating himself—just the thing for a long train trip. He sells a few of his CDs every day, and sometimes he stops off in towns along the way and picks up a couple of gigs. Still, he finds time to return to Toledo and play in the town folk festival the first Sunday in August and in the Wednesday street market in the summer.

Toledo isn't all the way back yet. Its beauty has to be searched out, on a misty morning along the river, in a room in a 1924 hotel or standing on a hill overlooking a gung ho paper mill.

The Basics: The newly renovated Yaquina Bay Hotel is the place to stay here. Chef's Place near the Alder Street arts district is a good local restaurant.

Reedsport

4,300

The Road: Oregon 38 takes off from Drain near Interstate 5 about forty miles south of Eugene and follows the Umpqua River for most of the way. It is one of Oregon's most beautiful road trips and offers a scenic prelude to Reedsport. In a state of abundant rivers, their variety and glorious beauty, the Umpqua stands out, wide and serene, passing through a lush green landscape and revealing new beauties at every turn.

Reedsport is all about water, but you wouldn't know it from the road. It's a blue-collar mill town, or it was before the timber industry caved in and the mills departed. The highway commercial strip cuts right through it and it's not a pretty sight—a strung-out hodgepodge of motels, worn shopping centers, and seaside clutter.

You can put the town in perspective by driving up Crestview Drive and peering across vacant lots to a stunning sight below. In one direction, Schofield Creek, looking more like a river, curves through a green landscape of mountain, marsh, and meadow. In the other direction is one of Oregon's grandest views as the Smith and Umpqua rivers join before flowing into the ocean a couple of miles away.

Water made Reedsport. In 1850, the schooner *Bostonian* wrecked on the Umpqua River bar. Its cargo was salvaged and taken to the place that is now Gardiner, a mile or so downriver from Reedsport. Sawmills were built and the place became a busy lumber port. Its prosperity shows in the Gardiner cemetery, where the graves and monuments are terraced on a slope and reached by flights of stone steps. It wasn't until the early twentieth century that railroad construction in western Douglas County made Reedsport a bustling town.

The best way to start a day in Reedsport isn't to head for the ocean but to drive north on U.S. 101 in the early morning and turn right on Lower Smith River Road; then turn right on Southside Road and right on Otter Slough Road. Especially in the golden light of a spring or summer morning, it is a lovely place, teeming with wildlife and heavy with smells of marsh and foliage. Afterward, you can chow down with locals at Leona's Restaurant a few doors down from Safeway.

On holiday weekends, aggressive trucks pulling all-terrain vehicles pour into Winchester Bay, five miles south on the coast. Even if you don't own one of these screaming machines, it's fun to drive out Salmon Harbor Drive and watch kids and would-be kids execute twists and turns on the dunes. In the evenings, villages spring up in designated camping spots near the dunes. Residents rich and poor, young and old, occupy flimsy tents and palatial recreational vehicles. They build driftwood campfires and create a community where they probably have more in common with their neighbors than they do back home.

On a hill above this cacophony is the Umpqua River Lighthouse, which blasts light twenty miles out to sea from a hill above the dunes. There are also Coast Guard buildings at the site and a museum, but visitors will spend most of their time scanning the water for gray whales, which pass here, as many as thirty an hour, in late December and early January on their way south to the Mexico lagoons. They return in March, headed for their northern feeding grounds off Alaska.

Since the ocean defines this area, it seems appropriate to mention a bar and an art gallery that are at least distantly water related. The Gardiner business district has pretty much been wiped out since International Paper closed its Gardiner mill. Nearly alone on the stretch of U.S. 101 that passes through town is Tsunami, a gallery where sculptor Mack Holman displays his works and those of other artists. The most unusual of these are hangings crafted of oiled kelp created by artist Ursula Dittl. They display beautifully on a wall but look as if they would revert to seaweed if left out in the rain.

Less artistic but rich with fishing vibes is the Oasis Lounge, a few blocks from the Winchester boat basin. Most visitors prefer the outdoors to this dark joint, but on Friday and Saturday nights, it features live music. One holiday weekend, the band was Stampede, a country-rock group from Coos Bay. The band's signature song is "Invincible," a word that catches the area's flavor—fun loving and hanging in there.

The Basics: There are Mexican and Chinese restaurants in Reedsport and several fish places in Winchester. Leona's Restaurant a few doors down from Safeway is a pleasant spot for breakfast. One of the better reasonably priced motels is the Salty Seagull.

Charleston
4,000

The Road: Charleston is just south of the town of Coos Bay and can be reached from the north on U.S. 101 and then cutting across North Bend to Empire Boulevard/Cape Arago Highway. From the south, a scenic route is to follow 101 and leave it at Beaver Hill Road. Proceed on that to Seven Devils Road and continue to Charleston.

In Charleston, where the ocean meets Coos Bay, rough little vessels rumble in and out of the boat basin to fish for crab, salmon, bottom fish, halibut, and tuna. Unlike most ports on the Oregon coast, it is still more a fishing than a tourist place. Fisherfolk psych themselves up with eggs and hashbrowns at the Basin Cafe in the boat basin before trudging to their boats and heading out over the bar. Water is all around and there are few places in Oregon where you feel more at the mercy of the weather. On stormy days, big, mean-looking clouds lounge at the horizon waiting to swagger in and kick the town around. On spring days, the sun lays a platinum sheath on the calm water.

The bay forms one of Oregon's most breathtaking marine environments, a grandly curving estuary that extends about nine miles and makes a U around the cities of North Bend and Coos Bay. Bar crossings can be perilous but the crossing into Coos Bay is one of the safest in the Northwest, partly because of its depth and partly because of the length of the jetties.

To get to know the place, get a room near the boat basin at Captain John's Motel, which is a clean, no-frills place. Time and money permitting, charter a boat at Betty Kay Charters or one of the other charter operators. Even if you don't fish, Betty

61

Kay can take you on a splendid bay or whale-watching cruise. Eat breakfast at the Basin Cafe, and at night have a drink at the Basin Inn adjacent to the café, where customers convivially banter and sling down drinks.

The beauty and fecundity of the water environment is explored at the South Slough Estuarine Reserve, five miles south of Charleston on Seven Devils Road. The reserve, which covers about seven square miles, studies the estuary, where saltwater and freshwater meet. This creates special conditions for life and great variety of environment: open waters, freshwater and salt marshes, swamps, sandy beaches, mud and sand flats, tidal pools, and sea grasses. The interpretive center is well organized and the staff extremely helpful. It's also a take-off point for the Hidden Creek Watershed Trail, which crosses an entire watershed ecosystem.

Farther south, off Cape Arago Highway, is Cape Arago Lighthouse, which is still imposing despite the U.S. Coast Guard's regrettable decision to pull the plug and leave it dark. Like lighthouses everywhere, Cape Arago was a symbol of caring and security, blasting light into the watery darkness.

We all love the ocean more when it serves up a good meal. For that, visit Charleston on the second Saturday in February for the annual Charleston Merchants Association Crab Feed. The Charleston crab feed is cousin to similar events in Elgin and Halfway, both hundreds of miles away in Eastern Oregon. Crab and the sea tie the state together, even if it's water on one side and sagebrush on the other. A thousand or so locals and visitors attend the event and consume close to a ton of crab along with coleslaw, bread, and baked beans.

And then there's Lynn Clarke, a man whose business is so far removed from waves, crab, and flopping fish that it seems to have been airlifted in by mistake. Clarke owns Boat Basin Plaza, a women's clothing and gift shop just off Cape

62

Arago Highway on Boat Basin Drive. It is to the boat basin as fireworks are to church—out of place but too flashy to ignore. He fills the rooms of his store with *bibelots* and *tschotkes*: a plastic dish of fettuccini Alfredo, heavily cosmeticized fish, art glass chandeliers. Backrooms are crammed with glittering women's clothing perfect for weddings, class reunions, and cruises.

Clarke opened the store in 1995 and says it has paid for a million-dollar home in Coos Bay and two Rolls Royce Corniche convertibles. Local women describing the place say, "You've gotta see it," and then laugh. I don't know what happens when the crowd at the Basin Inn stops by. They probably tell their friends about it, and they come in too.

The Basics: Captain John's Motel is clean, comfortable, and no-frills, but it is best to pay for one of the higher-priced rooms in the main building. Another good choice is Campbell's Vacation Apartments on Cape Arago Highway, which has views of the marina, the ocean, and the bar crossing. The Basin Cafe is a good place for breakfast and the Portside is a well-known seafood restaurant.

63

Myrtle Point

2,500

The Road: Myrtle Point can be reached coming from the east
or west on Oregon 42, an eighty-five-mile road that connects
Interstate 5 with U.S. 101 on the Oregon coast. It's a pretty drive,
part of it along the Middle Fork of the Coquille River.

Myrtle Point is a downer at first sight. It's bound to be. From either
direction on Oregon 42 unfolds a tapestry of tall trees, rushing
water, and tranquil valleys, but when the road hits Myrtle
Point it becomes a jangly business strip.

The Pacific Ocean is only twenty-five miles away, but this is
a blue-collar timber town, a place where cedar and Douglas fir
were cut up in local mills, and a thriving downtown supplied
workers' clothes, furniture, and a pint after work. In the late
nineteenth century, boat building and commerce up and down
the Coquille River made it a prosperous, even sophisticated
place. Its Victorian homes, festooned with gingerbread
millwork, still command residential neighborhoods.

Today's Myrtle Point has lost its gloss. Empty storefronts
line the gray business district on Spruce Street. Some of the
businesses have moved out onto the highway and some just
died. What remains are a few pieces of a real downtown: a
newspaper, the *Myrtle Point Herald,* a Mexican restaurant,
hardware stores, and a furniture emporium.

Even so, retirees and telecommuters trickle in, drawn by the
mild climate and the hauntingly lovely natural setting in the
Coquille Valley, lush with myrtle groves, rich dairy farms, and
the constant presence of water, mirroring forests and barns,
gushing down hillsides, pushing through river channels. Even
the local motel, the Myrtle Trees, has a view. In the winter,

64

water fills the wetlands just beyond the motel. In summer, water recedes and water lilies float on glassy ponds. The owners have placed picnic tables and a barbecue on the edge of the property to allow guests to drink in the view.

Any newcomer to town will be intrigued by a curving white dome topped by a cupola—a touch of exoticism in such a practical place. The combination looks something like the dome of a Russian Orthodox church placed flat on the ground. This wonderful flight of fancy was built in 1910 as a sanctuary by members of the Reorganized Church of Jesus Christ of Latter Day Saints, an offshoot of the Mormons. The architect had visited Salt Lake City and aspired to recreate the glorious acoustics of the Mormon Tabernacle. But the acoustics in the small, round building were terrible and the church and several subsequent owners had to abandon it. It is now a logging museum, surely the most unlikely small-town museum structure in the Northwest.

Acoustics don't matter much in a museum, although in this one they are so fractured that they become a curiosity. The museum displays some fine old logging machinery, but the exhibit that sets it apart is a collection of nine panels showing scenes of logging life, carved in deep relief on slabs of myrtlewood. A diesel mechanic, Ben Warnock, carved them, exquisitely rendering chain links, tree branches, and a man's hand on a woman's rear in a bar scene.

For the museum hungry, there's another one at the Coos County Fairgrounds, which are located in Myrtle Point. It's something like a consignment museum and anyone— other museums, tribes, local governments, and businesses— can create displays. Leaving the museum's contents to the generosity of outsiders can result in curious and unique exhibits, such as the scale model of the paper mill at Gardiner on the coast fifty miles away that was torn down in 2006. The intriguingly detailed model was more than a toy and was used to help manage the sprawling mill.

Once museums have been investigated and Victorian houses viewed, the real charm of Myrtle Point can be enjoyed. Drive or bike into the countryside, past grazing cows and puddle lakes, farms and barns, hills brushed with clouds, and a few shack estates, piled so high with mossy motor homes and junked cars that they're an art form.

And one of the best ways to enjoy a small town is to attend a meeting. It can be anything—city council, planning commission, or Chamber of Commerce. You don't need to talk or contribute, just listen. It's a window on a way of life that few outsiders see and sometimes you can even buy lunch.

On a Friday at noon in early February, the Myrtle Point Chamber of Commerce assembled at the Kozy Kitchen. These are optimistic folks, devoted to their town and enthusiastic about its prospects. They wouldn't belong to the chamber if they weren't. There were plans for a big chamber-sponsored event, talk about the chamber's Web site and of perhaps offering wireless Internet downtown. None of it would shake the earth off its axis, but for anyone with an affection for small towns, it was reassuring. They take pride in their town and appreciate what they have—nice company for lunch.

The Basics: The Myrtle Trees Motel is clean, comfortable, and reasonably priced. It also has its own little park with picnic tables and lovely view.

Powers

730

The Road: The fastest way to reach Powers is to take Oregon 42 from Interstate 5 south of Roseburg and continue fifty miles to the Powers turnoff. There also are beautiful routes over the mountains that connect Powers to the Interstate 5 corridor, but they should not be attempted in winter. It's best to consult the Powers Ranger Station for maps and road information.

You won't stumble upon Powers if you don't intend to go there. It's a speck on the map buried in forested mountains on a little-traveled road in the Coast Range. It seems one of the most secluded of Oregon towns, although it's not that remote. Coos Bay to the west is within commuting distance and Roseburg on the I-5 corridor is about eighty miles. Summer and fall are the best times to visit. Skies are clear, forested mountains that loom above the town are swept of clouds and mist, and golden light dapples the woods. But the winter too is gray-green and lovely. Big wet clouds settle on the town and creep through the hills in long, exploring arms.

Mornings, people gravitate to Jack's for coffee and breakfast. It's a warm spot with a plate-glass view of the street, not that there's that much to see in the downtown: a thrift shop, a well-stocked grocery store, and a restaurant. At night, the Powers Tavern and Cafe is a dim refuge warmed by a big stone fireplace. Outside, the smoke of dozens of wood fires settles on the town. Wood is plentiful here. Householders find blown-down trees in the forest that can be two hundred feet or so in length and get a firewood permit to cut them up and cart them home.

North Carolinians settled in the Powers area in the 1850s and the Wanger House, built of hand-hewn timbers probably in the 1870s, survives as a museum. The timber industry supported the town for years, but the Georgia-Pacific veneer mill closed in the early 1970s and the town began losing altitude. There's no movie theater in Powers, no shopping arcade, no skateboard park for the kids. It does have an excellent park that Coos County recycled from the paper mill site. A town twenty times the size of Powers would be well served with its pond, tennis court, and lush planting.

Recycling is a recurrent theme in Powers. Every year on the second Saturday of June, the town holds a community yard sale. Bargain hunters come from the coast, from Roseburg, and even from out-of-state to browse discards sold by dozens of local vendors. But most people with a day or two to spend in Powers will pass up the sale and head for the town's gorgeous surroundings: the South Fork of the Coquille River, the falls and creeks that feed it, the towering stands of old growth in the Rogue River-Siskiyou National Forest, the dizzying views of mountains and canyons, and the world's largest Port Orford cedar.

68   At Powers Ranger Station outside town, the district ranger hands out maps, tour pamphlets, and a highly informative guide explaining the geology of waterfalls along the river. Closest of these is Elk Creek Falls, only six miles from town starting on County Road 219. It's a short walk from the road to a rock canyon cut by a stream gushing around tumbled boulders. Golden light filters into the canyon, tipping leaves and brushing dense clumps of ferns. A nearby trail leads to a Port Orford cedar, which, at 239 feet, is the world's largest. This is a long slog up a switchback trail, and an easier way is to backtrack a short distance, turn on Forest Service Road 3358,

and continue about four and a half miles to a sign pointing to the tree observation site.

Some may believe that Powers will slide gradually into decay and abandonment. My prediction is that, in about twenty years, this rustic little place will be spiffed up possibly beyond recognition. At least one bistro will offer contemporary cuisine; there will be art galleries downtown and possibly a brewpub. Someone will purchase the ramshackle old Powers Hotel at the end of Second Avenue and turn it into artists' lofts. Artists will flock to the place, drawn by the lovely setting, the atmosphere of an era past, and the sense of living off the main road. Let's hope the locals profit.

The Basics: Jack's Cafe and Fountain is a warm, sunny gathering spot, particularly for breakfast. Across the street, the Northwoods Country Inn is a little more upscale. The Powers Tavern and Cafe is also a warm spot on a chilly evening. Finding a room for the night in Powers can take sharp eyes. Rooms are often available on the second floor of the Northwoods Country Inn. Powers County Park on the edge of town rents three one-room cabins with heat and lights for thirty dollars a night.

69

Gold Beach

2,400

The Road: U.S. 101 passes through Gold Beach about thirty-five miles north of the California border. Traveling south on Interstate 5, the most dependable route is to leave the Interstate at Grants Pass, continue south on U.S. 199 into California and connect to 101 near Crescent City. The detour into another state allows a glimpse of redwood forests and a lovely drive along the Smith River. The road continues along the coast, which becomes more dramatic as it crosses the state line back into Oregon.

Gold Beach on the southern Oregon coast feels more like a river town than an ocean place. The wild, tumbling Rogue River empties here, and given the choice between a walk on the sand or taking a jet boat one hundred and four miles into interior of Oregon, most visitors take the latter. The town's main drag is a highway strip lined with a wall of signs and motels that date it to the mid 1950s. Actually, Gold Beach dates from the 1850s when the first white settlers arrived and found gold in the sand where the Rogue meets the ocean. The pioneer cemetery off Second Street contains over three hundred graves, the earliest dating to 1859. The gold rush gave way to a salmon rush, and for years commercial fisheries and canneries flourished. Towering over the town even today is the spirit of R. D. Hume, an entrepreneur who arrived in 1876, established a salmon cannery, and soon dominated the local salmon industry. His legacy remains dramatically visible, although the canneries closed years ago.

If there is one sight to see in Gold Beach aside from the Rogue River and the ocean breaking on the sands, it is a ship,

70

the *Mary D. Hume*, that lists rotting and half-submerged in the Port of Gold Beach marina. Hume had the ninety-six-foot schooner built in Gold Beach—or Ellensburg as it was called then—in 1881 and named it after his wife. The ship ran up and down the Pacific coast until 1889, when it was converted to a whaler and sent to the Arctic. It prowled the frigid waters for years, and once brought a cargo of whale oil and baleen to San Francisco that is believed to be the most valuable whaling cargo ever taken. The ship also set a record for its six-and-a-half-year voyage in the Arctic, the longest ever undertaken by a whaling vessel. Hair-raising tales were told of hardship endured and death.

Later, as a tugboat, it hauled logs on Puget Sound. When it returned under its own power to Gold Beach in 1978, it was believed to have had the longest record of service of any vessel in the Northwest. The story then becomes a tragedy of bungled opportunities and legal scuffles. The Curry Historical Society acquired the vessel and planned to lift it into a cradle and restore it. The lifting failed, a hole was punched into the vessel's hull, and it sank. The society advertised it for sale. A New Jersey man showed interest, and after a legal battle, acquired title to the *Mary D. Hume*. The boat was never restored, and with its spiritual cargo of human misery, triumph, and dogged longevity it sits on the bottom of the marina in water to its deck.

It's considered the most-photographed structure in Gold Beach and it may be the only half-sunken vessel in America that is a genuine tourist attraction. Someday, however, the smokestack will disintegrate and the whole structure will collapse into the water. When that happens a local wit suggests that the city buy another old boat and sink it. It would be nice to see the *Mary D. Hume* restored. But then again, the ghostly ship lying in the water just a short distance from where it was

71

built, peeling, decaying, its black portholes staring blindly toward the bustling marina, may be more evocative than if it were raised, restored, and polished.

For an uplifting alternative to this wondrous and depressing saga, drive thirteen miles north to the Prehistoric Gardens, where the neck of a brachiosaur rises unnervingly from the trees. The gardens are one of America's great roadside attractions, dating from the era of Burma Shave signs. They are the creation of E. V. Nelson, who harbored an interest in dinosaurs, and in 1953 found the twenty-five-acre site, dense with Port Orford cedar, Sitka spruce, Douglas fir, rhododendrons, huckleberry, and native fern.

He set out to create a community of dinosaurs from steel frames and cement. The twenty-three creatures he imagined came vividly alive, including a winged pteranodon, tyrannosaurus rex, a triceratops, pterodactyl, and the brachiosaur. The latter took two years to build and stands forty-six feet tall. The great beasts would be impressive anywhere but the setting in an Oregon rain forest makes them eerily awe inspiring. Better than in any jurassicized movie, they inhabit their home, stomping on vines and ferns in a primeval forest, sun slanting through towering trees. If only for a walk, it is an enchanting place.

72

The Basics: There are lots of good motels and restaurants in Gold Beach. The Azalea is a clean, comfortable, and reasonably priced motel. There are other places where an ocean view can be had for more money. A lot more money will buy a room at Tu Tun Lodge, one of Oregon's premier resorts, seven miles inland on the Rogue River.

Southern Oregon

Southern Oregon

Eugene

Bend

126

5

58

20

Oakland
Sutherlin
138

Christmas
Valley

Roseburg

42

230

97

31

395

Wolf
Creek

227

Grants
Pass

Rogue
River

Shady Cove

234

Paisley

199

Gold
Hill

Medford

62

140

Cave Junction
Takilma

Klamath Falls

Lakeview

140

Miles
0   25   50   100

Sutherlin
7,700
Oakland
950

The Road: The most scenic way to reach Sutherlin coming from the north is to leave Interstate 5 south of Cottage Grove on Oregon 99, pass through Drain, and continue west on Oregon 38 to Elkton. Then take Oregon 138 east to Tyee Road and turn right. This is an exquisite drive through a forested canyon along the Umpqua River. At Fort McKay Road, turn left and continue into Sutherlin. At each turn of the road and bend in the river, a different, more ravishing view emerges.

The beauty of the land around Oakland and Sutherlin must lodge in the psyche of the people who live there. The gushing rivers and deep green forests are an everyday part of life, and the worth of that kind of amenity can't be estimated. Sutherlin's gateway is an off-ramp on Interstate 5, the traffic river that flows from Mexico to Canada. Signs announce fuel, lodging, and road food, but the real town is on Central Avenue, well beyond this confusion of neon.

The business district is a two-mile commercial strip lined with low, boxy structures housing cafés, shops, and even a plywood plant, rebuilt after a 2005 fire. About seventy-five hundred people live here in the heart of Southern Oregon. It's a nice friendly place but short on charm. Sutherlin left that for Oakland, a sister city three miles to the north where the business district has been preserved in all its nineteenth-century red-brick solidity.

Anyone passing through Sutherlin on a regular basis learns to stop at Digger Don's Diner just off Central Avenue. It's a classic small-town café, plain and unpretentious, with cheery waitresses, strong coffee, and good food made from scratch. The owner, Don Reed, serves big portions—perhaps to a fault. His Giant Angus Burger is a five-pound hamburger served on a bun the size of a pillow, topped with tomatoes and a half head of shredded lettuce accompanied by a big pile of fries. He picks up the check for anyone who can consume the entire five-pounder (that's everything on the plate, including bun, lettuce, and fries) at one sitting. Many have tried but only twenty succeeded. Pinned to the wall are snapshots in a Hall of Fame of weakly smiling people who finished one of these humongous sandwiches.

A good first stop in any small town is the Chamber of Commerce, where maps and brochures describing area attractions are available. Next stop is the local newspaper, if only to buy the latest edition. In Sutherlin, it's the *North County News*, which claims its pages offer Real People/Real News. Becky Holm, the editor, packs it with columns and essays by local writers and thorough listings of town happenings. She will probably offer travel tips if she's not on deadline.

The newspaper shares space with Books Gallery, overseen by Cheryl Owens, who maintains a stock of good-quality used books including an extensive local history section. Next stop might be Digger Don's Rockhound Haven and the Mystical Oasis Dance Studio, both in the same building. The owner is the same Don Reed who owns the diner. He loves digging stones—hence the name Digger Don.

Don proudly shows his rocks: opals, purple charoite, laramar, lapis lazuli, plume agate, stedonite, and glassy black fire obsidian. He turns the stones into pendants, necklaces, and earrings. His wife, Mezdulene, helps him out in the rock shop but her passion is belly dancing and she devotes her Mystical Oasis Dance Studio to the art. Blond and zaftig, she teaches belly dancing and judges competitions in Sutherlin and around the United States. She also publishes a magazine, *Jareeda*, devoted to belly dancing.

By this time, it's mid-afternoon and time for a short car trip through time. Drive out Central Avenue to Old Pioneer Road, turn left and wind three miles through white oak, fir, and incense cedar to the outskirts of Oakland. The town began in 1851 with a grist mill. In anticipation of the railroad's arrival in 1872, the old town picked up, buildings and all, and moved about a mile to its present location. At the turn of the nineteenth century, it was the biggest turkey-shipping center in the western United States and the broad-breasted bronze turkey was developed here. But the turkey industry crashed during World War II and local agriculture also suffered. Perhaps because the town slumbered, it retained its nineteenth-century character. Handsome brick structures built in the 1880s and 1890s using locally made brick line the city's two-block business district, and over eighty properties in the city were built between 1852 and 1890. The town has a museum feel, much different than Sutherlin's offhand energy, but it's visually pleasing, and offers a few restaurants and a good museum.

After an hour or two of sightseeing, it's time for a drink at the Oakland Tavern, a warm western bar where customers play darts and banter over beers. The walls are red brick and a big red neon Michelob sign hangs near the door. Afterward, you can return to Sutherlin on County Road 388, which passes just outside.

Evenings, downtown Sutherlin goes mostly dark, but if you are lucky enough to be there on the first or third Thursday of the month, Mezdulene Reed presents a belly dance dinner show at the diner. Her students shimmy, shake, and undulate in brilliantly colored chiffons and satins. Sinuous North African music accompanies the show, although Mezdulene would like to vary it with something like "I Wanna See You Bellydance" by the Russian rokenrol group, Red Elvises. Alas, she cannot do so in a cabaret without paying vexing fees, but you can hear it from the street on nights when belly dance classes are taught at the dance studio. In downtown Sutherlin, it pushes multiculturalism to new levels.

The Basics: The Umpqua Regency Inn off the Sutherlin freeway off-ramp offers spacious, well-equipped rooms. For a town this size, the dining choices are remarkably varied. Digger Don's is open for breakfast, lunch, and dinner and serves prime rib on Fridays. The local Abby's Pizza draws a big crowd of locals for its hearty, inexpensive breakfasts. There are Mexican and Chinese restaurants and an Italian restaurant, Pedotti's, which has a large traditional Italian menu. Migado serves Korean, Japanese, and American food. The Chamber of Commerce Visitor Information Center is on Central Avenue about two blocks east of Interstate 5.

Wolf Creek
700

The Road: Traveling from the north or south on Interstate 5, take exit 76 twenty miles north of Grants Pass. A more scenic route traveling from the south is to leave I-5 the Merlin exit (exit 61) a few miles north of Grants Pass and continue on Merlin Road through Merlin. Take Merlin-Galice Road through Galice and Rand and then Lower Grave Creek Road, and Lower Wolf Creek Road into Wolf Creek. This is a lovely drive at all times of the year, especially in winter and late spring when shredded clouds snag on spiky hills.

A woman who owned a business overlooking Interstate 5 in the vicinity of Wolf Creek saw many rare and wonderful sights as they rocketed past. One that stuck was a large van from which protruded the heads and necks of two live giraffes. The Southern Oregon Visitors Association might consider that image for its logo.

Southern Oregon is a rich stew of cultures and ways of life. Begin with Oregon logging tradition, built on a bedrock of pioneer values. Add a little California New Age, a touch of apocalyptic paranoia, and the fragrant remains of 1960s hippie idealism, now curdled a bit. This is layered on a lovely green countryside spread over craggy slopes and contorted valleys, quite unlike the placid Willamette Valley.

Hippie communes began arriving in Southern Oregon in the late 1960s. As these experiments in twentieth-century tribalism broke apart, another wave of outsiders flowed into Southern Oregon. Among them were conservative survivalists, relationship adventurers, and several gay and lesbian communes. They found snug dens in the forested hills

79

and valleys around Wolf Creek, which was once a stage stop and continued as a small service center for locals and a gas stop on the interstate. Last count, it had two markets, two gas stations, and the Wolf Creek Inn.

The Inn was built in 1883 as a stage stop on the route between Roseburg and Redding. The Oregon Parks and Recreation Department owns it now and offers impeccably restored and maintained rooms at reasonable prices and also a good restaurant.

Lanes and canyons spread out from Wolf Creek like fault lines in cracked glass and it helps to see it all from above. In the morning after the fog lifts, take off from the Inn toward Interstate 5 south. Just before the on-ramp, turn right on Bridge Lane and continue to a sign that announces London Peak up what appears an impassable dirt road. The road is well maintained but too narrow and winding for some nervous systems. Continue on the road and, when it forks, veer to the right and continue up County Road 33-6-26. At the top follow a trail that leads to an overlook furnished with a bench and contemplate a sweeping vista. Far below, Interstate 5 curves around a bend toward the timber towns of Glendale, Riddle, and Roseburg. Valleys and meadows are spread along the highway, and little lanes and canyons burrow off it into the plush green hills. Descending from this aerie, turn back toward town and take Coyote Creek Road, which leads deep into the hills to the gold-rush ghost town of Golden with its 1892 carpenter Gothic church.

To head in another direction physically and politically, pass through town and follow Wolf Creek Road about four and a half miles. A driveway on the left crosses over Wolf Creek and ends at a meadow at the foot of hills forested with Douglas fir, madrone, bigleaf maple, and white oak and dotted with a few hippie-rustic cabins. This is the Wolf Creek Sanctuary, property of Nomenus, a non-profit religious organization run by the San Francisco-based Radical Faeries. Local caretakers call it a "Queer-Pagan Retreat Center."

Queer pagans have been meeting here since the mid-1970s when it began as a "sissy-Maoist" commune. Nomenus now holds the property and sponsors three gatherings each year that can draw several hundred people for "faggot-oriented spirituality, community and collectivity, living in harmony with the Beings around us, and subject-subject consciousness." In 1979, the commune was firebombed by a disgruntled local who didn't like the residents' penchant for cross dressing and various other transgressions. But Nomenus now is much more incorporated into the community of Wolf Creek, and residents work in local businesses and get involved in town projects.

Nomenus Wolf Creek Sanctuary is listed in the phone book, and if you call in advance, they will invite you out, gay or straight. The residents are cordial and spiritual and will more likely be seen digging ditches than cross dressing, although the latter is always a possibility. They may show you their barn, vegetable gardens, altars, and holy sites where they commune with the gods and spirits of the dead. They could also invite you to their communal residence, a warmly convivial place where the talk leaps from gossip to spirituality to farming.

81

Not known for a vibrant retail scene, Wolf Creek's "downtown" still has evolved over the years. The Wolf Creek Store was built in 1881 and enlarged in 1910. Today, it serves as a general store, message center, hangout, and smokers' porch. Newer to the scene is Circle of Wolves, a gallery and gift shop selling crystals, jewelry, and art objects with an emphasis on the mystical. It also includes a little bar much patronized by Nomenus residents that serves wine and craft beers.

The owners, Karen Schilberg and Nancy Johnston, align themselves with pagan thought and they are deeply involved in the community, which in spite of its counterculture overlay is still a little Oregon blue-collar town. Johnston moved to Wolf Creek thirty years ago when she and her husband bought a deserted hippie commune. Like the town, she is evolving.

"I thought when we moved here we would be pillars of the community, and now we are," she says.

The Basics: The Wolf Creek Inn is a fine place to stay provided you enjoy simple rooms without flounces and furbelows. For a working-class escape from this genteel hostelry, travel about nine miles north to Glendale and find your way to the town center and the Glendale Village Inn. It has a restaurant and a good bar built of huge timbers from an old mill and hung with logging equipment and saws.

Gold Hill
1,080
Rogue River
2,085

The Road: Rogue River is two miles east of Grants Pass just off Interstate 5. Gold Hill nearby can also be reached directly from the freeway, but it's more scenic to pass through Rogue River and take North River Road beginning on the east edge of town.

It's best to head for the towns of Gold Hill and Rogue River in Southern Oregon in deep summer when a lazy haze slips across the landscape. Coming from the north, there is a point on Interstate 5 where the world changes. I pinpoint it at the Douglas County line a few miles south of Cottage Grove. The softly rounded hills of the Willamette Valley turn sharp and choppy there and laurel, oak, and pine mat the landscape.

The towns, about ten miles apart, lie on the Rogue, a river that turns placid, then raucous as it winds across southwestern Oregon. They couldn't be called sister cities—cousins maybe. Rogue River, with a few more than two thousand residents, is about twice the size of Gold Hill and appears a lot more prosperous. It has a fine arboretum, the Palmerton, with a new footbridge that crosses Evans Creek. Just outside town, the new Depot Street Bridge arches over the Rogue, connecting the town to a park, a boat launch, and an excellent motel.

Gold Hill's got no fancy bridge and no excellent motel. It reclines by the river like a guy who's out of work and likes it that way. It has its origins in a gold strike in the vicinity in 1853 and takes its name from a mountain northeast of the city where the Gold Hill lode was discovered. Rogue River,

83

under another name, started as a ferry across the Rogue. Both towns offer excellent small museums that recount their towns' histories.

For a weekend of the weird and wonderful, start in Rogue River. If you are staying at the Best Western, walk over to Karen's Kitchen, a warm little place where people huddle over morning coffee and friendly waitresses offer chicken-fried steak as a breakfast special. Next stop might be the Woodinville Museum, housed in an early-twentieth-century home. Volunteers maintain the place fastidiously and are warmly solicitous in explaining its contents. These include a quilt sewn of tobacco pouches and a unique finger painting in the style of Monet that was created by children who applied thousands of paint dots with their fingertips. If asked, the volunteers will recommend local attractions, including Pholia Farm, ten miles from Rogue River near the town of Wimer on West Evans Creek Road.

A retiree from the U.S. Marines, Vern Caldwell, and his wife, Gianaclise, started the farm in 2003, stocking it with Nigerian dwarf goats, which produce rich, high-protein milk, ideal for making cheese. The animals are lovingly and laboriously cared for. They are prolific breeders, which means that Gianaclise has become a skilled goat midwife. In their barn, cushioned with hay and monitored by huge, caring dogs, they look more like pets than farm animals. The Caldwells produce only about three hundred pounds of cheese a month, but it's of superb quality and sold in New York, Chicago, and Portland.

It's only a few miles from Pholia to the Wimer Way Cafe, a local institution where a former Rogue River chief of police presides. It's a good stop for coffee or lunch and a jump-off point for a lovely scenic road that loops through canyons, meadows, and mountains along a gushing creek and comes out at Gold Hill. To reach it, continue through Wimer and follow Evans Creek Road out of town. Turn right at Meadows Road and right on Oregon 234.

Compared to Rogue River with its nicely ordered downtown and air of civic pride, Gold Hill has a raw, nailed-together feel. Its old houses haven't been gussied up much and it's easy to imagine the place as it might have been in gold-rush days. Outside town there's a winery, Del Rio Vineyards, housed in an 1865 hotel and stage stop. And farther out on Sardine Creek Road is the Oregon Vortex. Whether you believe this is a mystery of nature or a carnival-style sucker trap, it is fun and the staff explain it with great conviction.

Owners claim that it has been a place of eerie happenings since before the arrival of the white man. There's a shack, once an assay office for the Gray Eagle Mine, where weird changes in perspective occur. A ball appears to roll uphill, and people change size mysteriously. A laborious theory is offered to explain these anomalies that involves a "spherical field of force" that can bend light and even cause objects to grow and shrink. Others say it's all an optical illusion.

If it's late in the day, the more venturesome might stop at one of the Gold Hill saloons. Overheard conversations can be hair raising and everyone seems to style their hair in braids or ponytails, and not because they are hippies. Still the bar scene here has a kinder, gentler feel than that of many big-city wine bars.

Returning to Rogue River on River Road, a moment of surprise and disorientation occurs, and this moment will probably be more intense in the future. On a hill near the road, only a short distance from Interstate 5, at a place where deer come down to graze, rises a vision of golden onion domes and a Russian icon the size of a house painted on the side of a blue building. It's St. Innocent Russian Orthodox Church, spiritual home of about fifty people in the vicinity and led by Father Seraphim Cardoza, a Russian Orthodox priest. The church, which was remodeled from a barn in the late 1990s, is being dismantled now and will be replaced by a new, larger sanctuary, also designed with onion domes and an imposing icon.

There's no denying the strangeness of these buildings, appearing in a place not far from the California border and near an interstate highway. But in southern Oregon, they fit in better than they would in other Oregon locales. There's something about the Southern Oregon milieu that inspires the pursuit of dreams.

The Basics: In Gold Hill, the Lazy Acres Motel and RV Park offers four clean, inexpensive rooms and the Guadalajara across the railroad tracks on Fourth Street is a popular Mexican restaurant. In Rogue River, the Best Western Inn at the Rogue offers comfortable, spacious rooms at a location near the river. Note that in directories and on the Web, it's usually listed with a Grants Pass address. Karen's Kitchen near the motel is well known for breakfasts and the Creekside Pub and Deli is popular for drinks and dinner.

Shady Cove
2,850

The Road: Shady Cove is easily reached from Interstate 5, taking Oregon 234 at Gold Hill twenty miles northeast to Oregon 62 and continuing a few miles north to Shady Cove. A more scenic route is to leave the freeway at Canyonville and take Oregon 227 through pretty forested country, joining Oregon 62 at Trail a few miles from Shady Cove.

Side-by-side, Shady Cove in Southern Oregon has one of Oregon's loveliest thoroughfares and one of its ugliest. The ugliest is the Oregon 62 commercial strip, which cuts right through town. It's a clutter of shops catering to tourists, a couple of restaurants and bars, and some rafting companies. It's possible to find riverside retreats, such as Bel Di's Restaurant, or a flavorful local business like Fishing Hole Fly Shop, but you have to look hard. The other thoroughfare is the Rogue River, which flows near the main drag, broad and green, pushing against forested banks. Rafting and fishing are the favorite sports here, and for a different water experience, there's Lost Creek Lake, about ten miles east of Shady Cove, where there are thirty miles of shoreline, with park sites, boat ramps, and a trail system.

87

Shady Cove was born and raised as a tourist town. It began as a summer home and camping area and later became a suburb for commuting millworkers. It wasn't incorporated as a city until 1972. To encounter anything that looks like history, you have to go to Trail—or what's left of Trail—a few miles outside Shady Cove. Trail's roots go back to the 1850s, when it was a transportation hub for Southern Oregon and points beyond. Later, it became a productive timber town.

The Upper Rogue at any time of the year is entrancing and Shady Cove offers an excellent jumping-off point. In the summer, from about May 15 to September 15, Rapid Pleasure Raft Rental, oldest of several local rafting companies, transports rafters ten miles up the river to a fish hatchery located below Lost Creek Dam, and leaves them to float for three or four hours back to Shady Cove. The river here also is famous for salmon, steelhead, and trout fishing. Casey State Park, ten miles northeast of Shady Cove, is a good place to start enjoying the river for fishing and boating.

If you yearn for a little shade, or even some less strenuous activity than fishing and rafting, the Trail Creek Tavern Museum might be enough to tear you away from the water. Begun in 1934, the tavern pumped suds to local loggers and built a reputation for rowdiness and general disrepute until New Years Eve 1996, when the Jackson County Sheriff pulled its license. The Upper Rogue Historical Society acquired the building and turned it into a museum, retaining the original bar where countless pints had been hoisted. The museum's exhibits are varied, but two stand out. One is a small collection of memorabilia relating to actress Ginger Rogers, who for fifty years owned Rogers Rogue River Ranch between Shady Cove and Eagle Point. Rogers drove around in a green Rolls Royce and appears to have been well liked in the area. Her mother Lela, one of the most formidable of all stage mothers, also resided at the ranch for a time. The other is a collection of three metal wagon-wheel rims, turned into works of art by an extraordinary machinist and welder, Carl Jantzer. Jantzer chose an assortment of the museum's collection of unusual tools, laid them on a welding table, and created designs with the tools that would fit into the space of a wagon wheel and then welded them together. It took not only extraordinary precision and welding ability, but a fine artist's eye to visualize an overall pattern made with the tools that could fit into the space. Among the tools are butcher knife, shovel, sickle, harpoon fork used to lift loose hay, a sheep shearer, and many other items.

The best time to experience the town, not the river, may be at night, when you can find romance and fun if you know where to look. Start at Bel Di's Restaurant in the heart of town on Oregon 62. It looks like a cluster of cottages and is actually a three-bedroom home that was remodeled into a restaurant in 1977. The menu, which is reasonably priced for this level of comfort, features a luxurious, slightly dated collection of steaks, seafood, and more complex preparations such as breaded veal cutlets and chicken marsala. Dinner can be served in the quiet dining room that overlooks the river or in the velvety-dim bar, which used to be a master bedroom. To get the adrenalin pumping after such tranquility, walk across the road to the Shady Cove Sports Bar, a boisterous, huggy kind of place, and enjoy or even participate in the karaoke on Wednesdays, Fridays, and some Saturday nights. Karaoke is created by playing what is usually a popular or well-known song, but leaving out the lead vocals. These are supplied by singers in the bar who dare to stand in front of everyone and wail their hearts out. Inevitably some of the singers are bad, some are OK, and a few are terrific. More than anything, in a small town, you get sense that the songs are sung with the gritty awareness that the songwriters intended. In Shady Cove, for sure, they sound like they're singing their lives.

89

The Basics: Shy's, a comfortable, off-hand café, is a good place for breakfast and there are Mexican, Chinese, and American-style restaurants. The Maple Leaf Motel offers spacious, attractive rooms at very reasonable prices. The Edgewater Inn is more expensive but it's right on the river and maintains a path, a fishing hole, and a boat launch for guests.

Cave Junction
1,700
Takilma

The Road: Cave Junction is thirty miles south of Grants Pass on U.S. 199. Take Oregon 46 at Cave Junction to reach Oregon Caves. Takilma and environs are south of Cave Junction. Follow the directions below.

One way to suggest the attitude and point of view of the Illinois Valley is to start with directions: to arrive at the Out 'n' About Treesort, follow U.S. 199 from Cave Junction south. Pass the lions, leopards, and tigers at Great Cats World Park, and continue about seven miles to Waldo Road. Then drive about six miles to Takilma Road and turn right. A little collection of odd houses and a trailer appears to the left. Continue past the blacksmith shop and the rusting buses that recall the psychedelic era, and turn left on Page Creek Road. Signs will guide you to the Treesort.

The Illinois Valley is in the southwest corner of Oregon, and like most corners, it attracts people who want to get out of the way. The rural scene reflects the laid-back way of life—a proliferation of shacks, mossy mobile homes, wrecked cars, and junk. There is a sense of amiable disregard for middle-class fastidiousness here and definitely it's a place where people nail together lives on the edge. The biggest town in the area is Cave Junction, which is strung out along the road near the junction of Oregon 46 and U.S. 199. It bills itself as the home of the Oregon Caves, twenty miles east of town. Guides lead tours throughout the day and explain stalactites, stalagmites, and flowrock. Water films the rock, drips from the ceiling, and lies in puddles on steep stone steps.

The caves can be experienced in a half-day, leaving time for some of the valley's less-evident attractions. This is when the above directions may help. They lead to Takilma, site of a major hippie influx, mostly from California, that began in the late 1960s. Takilma is not a town in the usual sense, but a collection of shacks and hippie-rustic architecture spread out for several miles off Takilma Road. Once, there were three communes here: The Meadows, Magic Forest, and Doo-Dah. They broke up over the years, leaving a scent of hippie incense that has never quite dissipated. One of the pleasures of a leisurely tour through Takilma and environs is meeting white-haired men and women who arrived in the 1960s and never left.

They have raised children, paid mortgages, and held jobs. They live in houses that feel as natural and organic as wool socks, retain a generally dour view of mainstream politics, and share a distrust of the Bureau of Land Management, which they fear for its tree-cutting policies. It's this distrust more than communalism that binds them now.

One way to tap into the spirit of the place is to tune in to the local Internet radio at www.takilmafm.com. It replaced a pirate low-power FM station that went off the air several years ago, evidently in fear of a Federal Communications Commission crackdown. This means you can't cruise through here with the radio blasting the world according to Takilma without carrying an Internet connection. Still, it pays to check out the site in advance for links to the local art scene, not to mention the music and interviews.

Rather than rock and rebellion, art now characterizes Takilma, but it has to be searched out. Local artisans, although cordial when approached, don't advertise much. Studios are hidden away behind trees and in buildings that look like L'il Abner just moved out.

You can start with Jim Rich's blacksmith shop, Takilma Forge and Wagon Works, at a bend on Takilma Road. When Rich isn't smithing, he plays baroque woodwind instruments in Jefferson Baroque Orchestra, which gives concerts in Ashland and Grants Pass. Not far from the blacksmith shop, Newman (the name he prefers) works in leather and creates *commedia dell'arte* and *carnivale* masks that he sells to theaters and colleges. He welcomes visitors by appointment.

Way up the road is Kendall Art Glass where glassblower David Kendall fashions glass ornaments, hummingbird feeders, lampshades, and other pieces. Across the meadow from Kendall's glassworks is a weathered wooden geodesic dome. Leo Goodman built it and he doesn't mind if visitors walk onto his property to admire it. He's a gnomish man, alert and curious, with a white partly braided beard. He came to Takilma in 1986 from Santa Cruz and met Mar, his wife-to-be, a few days after his arrival. They have lived the tragedies and joys of life here and remain gentle at heart and spiritual in approach.

In addition to his other projects, Goodman manages TakilmaFM, which he considers a moving work of art. Other works of art that he has had a hand in include a hay bale house built for an artist friend, Marjorie Reynolds, down the road, and a new house for himself and Mar, which is several stories high, built into a hillside, and oddly harmonious with its surroundings despite its size,

But to return to the Out 'n' About Treesort. Whether or not you stay there, it's a wonderful example of a kind of crazy daring that happens in the environs of Takilma and a few other places on the planet. It was conceived by Michael Garnier, who came to Takilma in 1972 to work for the local free clinic. He hungered to create a B&B, and when his efforts on the ground failed, he took to the trees. He built his first treehouse in 1990 and it took years before county officials would give him the permits he needed to expand. To illustrate its safety, he packed sixty-six people, two dogs, and a cat totaling 10,847 pounds into a treehouse eighteen feet above ground. Today, there are several units, including the Treezebo, which hangs thirty-seven feet in the air and includes a queen-size bed and two singles, toilet, sink, refrigerator, and chairs. Like its neighbors in Takilma, Out 'n' About is an organic place, growing like a rare vine, blossoms opening in the trees.

The Basics: The Treesort is the place to stay here if you don't mind trees and your vertigo is under control. There are also several lodges and inns in the vicinity. The Junction Inn in Cave Junction is large and comfortable but badly needs renovation.

Christmas Valley

1,000

The Road: The road to Christmas Valley takes off from Oregon
31, about seventy miles south of Bend. An immense rock
monolith, Fort Rock, announces the turn onto Fort Rock Road,
which leads to Christmas Valley-Wagontire Road and into
Christmas Valley.

The town of Christmas Valley doesn't so much appear as unroll
onto the landscape, farms first, then pole barns, a lot of prefab
houses, and some trailers. There's no town center here, it's
all off Christmas Valley Highway: a couple of grocery stores,
an A-frame lodge that may have been impressive in its day in
the early 1960s, an airstrip, a farm machinery business, and a
little pizza restaurant.

The question arises: what is this fairly sizable town doing
twenty-eight miles from the nearest main road? And why
does it look like it was built from the ground up in the last
few decades? And what to make of the lodge that could
accommodate a much larger tourist population than you can
see in these parts? And what about the motel on the lake,
where fat geese and ducks waddle up to guest units with lake
views, units that nonetheless look in need of some TLC?

The explanation is pretty simple. In the early 1960s, a
southern California land developer named Penn Phillips saw
this sagebrush-covered plain and decided it could be a desert
retirement and vacation community where vistas stretched to
far horizons, and intriguing geologic formations rose grandly
from the barren landscape.

He wasn't the first to be captivated by a vision of life on
the high desert. In the early 1900s, homesteaders descended

94

on nearby Fort Rock Valley, hoping to farm the land. They endured drought, alkaline soil, jackrabbits, and erosion but finally gave up. It wasn't until 1955 that electricity came to the valley and made it possible to pump the aquifers beneath the Fort Rock Basin and water fields of high-quality alfalfa.

Water made Phillips' vision possible. He laid out a townsite with Christmassy street names, such as Jingle Bell Road and Snowflake Lane, and created a water system, an artificial lake, a golf course, and the lodge. The lots sold quickly, often sight unseen. Purchasers who expected an Oregon haven of lush meadows, streams, and vistas of forested mountains weren't prepared for the arid high-desert terrain nor for the sub-zero winter temperatures. Few houses were ever built, but even now, years after the reality of life in Christmas Valley has sunk in, retirees arrive, drawn by cheap land, the austere high-desert scenery, and an amiable, countrified milieu.

On arrival, check in to the Lakeview Motel. The motel units from the outside appear in steep decline but they are clean, comfortable, and not overpriced. In the summer, the owners cook steak dinners on a barbecue behind the restaurant. Breakfast is served in the motel restaurant beginning at 5:30 a.m., and on Thursdays and Fridays, there's often an informal gun swap where guys in caps and cowboy hats trade rifles and whatever over coffee and eggs.

Shopping here is pretty much limited to the grocery store and a little gift shop, Forever Christmas, but geology is the real attraction. Fort Rock, a ring of bronze rock with a piece carved out of it, was formed when rising basalt magma hit a muddy lake bottom and created an explosion of pulverized magma. The magma fell back to create a ring of rock that was breached over the years as wave action in the ancient lake wore a chunk out of it. The rock circle has been likened to a ruined castle, an amphitheater, the Colosseum, and a citadel.

Whatever it reminds you of, it's majestic and evocative. Not far from the formation is the Fort Rock Valley Historical Homestead Museum, a melancholy collection of cabins and buildings erected by early-twentieth-century homesteaders and later abandoned.

Eight miles northwest, Hole-in-the-Ground, a five-hundred-foot-deep pit, looks like a meteor crater, but it too was formed when magma hit a lake bed. And eight miles north of Christmas Valley is Crack-in-the-Ground, a deep, narrow rift cutting two miles through basalt. In the same general area are the Christmas Valley sand dunes, eighty-nine hundred acres of ash and pumice that fell seven thousand years go when Mount Mazama erupted and created Crater Lake.

And then there are the zorses. Anyone who comes to Christmas Valley must have a touch of the individual or downright eccentric to live there, and meeting them is one of the pleasures of a visit to the valley. Jenny and Roger Stirnemann-Wilson came in 2001 from Philomath and founded Broken Spoke Mule Ranch, where they breed and sell mules. A sideline is a pair of zorses, the rare product of a zebra stallion and a horse mare.

96

These are not docile animals—they are independent, alert for danger (perhaps a lion creeping through the sagebrush), and hard to train. Their caramel and black striped coats are striking enough to bring travelers to a halt on Christmas Valley Road and their fame has extended all the way to London. Not long ago, the Stirnemann-Wilsons were surprised when a whacky London reality show, *Big Brother,* telephoned to talk about the zorses, which they had seen on the Internet. Roger handled them with much aplomb and to great applause from the audience of Londoners. The zany interview can be seen on the Web at http://www.youtube.com/watch?v=IYBxIlwEf3o. The spirit of Christmas Valley plays well in London.

The Basics: The Lakeview Motel is the place to stay here. The motel units on Baert Lake could use some renovation, but they are clean and reasonably comfortable. The café at the motel is the place for breakfast and the Lakeside Terrace Restaurant serves dinners. A pizza from Coyote Pizza, taken out and eaten on the edge of the lake, is also an option.

97

Paisley

250

The Road: Coming from the north on U.S. 97, pass through Bend and continue to the junction of Oregon 31. From there, it's a wide-open road along the edge of the Fremont National Forest and past Summer Lake, a shallow, alkaline body.

Try coming into Paisley in the late afternoon when the sun is setting and the light is softly golden on the sagebrush-matted hills of the Chewaucan Valley. Seen from the road, it's a tree-shaded rest stop—saloon, gas station, mercantile, café. A quick detour from the main road reveals a town with civic structure and tradition. There's a severe white Methodist Church, a columned, two-story school, a community center, and a two-story structure called the dorm. Farther out, the town unfolds into large lots, nice big houses, sometimes of eccentric design, fields, pastures, red barns, and bundled hay. It's a generous place, multicultural and rooted in a history that goes back generations since the area was settled by ranchers in the late 1860s.

98

Paisley would be flavorful at any time of the year, but for an outsider, it's best experienced during the Mosquito Festival, held the last full weekend in July. The event celebrates not the mosquito but its eradication. It began as a way to raise money to control the insects that invade the city in clouds from nearby marshes. For anyone who savors Western culture, this is the place to be. There's lots of lodging in the vicinity but make reservations early.

The town fills up with tourists, buckaroos, roadside vendors, and local ranchers. There's a parade, a rodeo, a barbecue, a pancake breakfast, and a big dance in the community center.

Local artists display their work and kids hang out at the fish pond most of the day for a fishing derby. Saturday afternoon, chuck roast cooked to melting fibers in a pit for thirteen hours is served at the school cafeteria with slaw, potato salad, and baked beans.

Even if Paisley can be walked end to end in ten minutes, it still helps to have someone point you in the right direction. If you're lucky, it will be Larry Duckworth. Early morning, he can be found over a cup of coffee at the Homestead Restaurant. Otherwise, he's at his bait and tackle business, the Fisher King's Fly Shop. He's a leathery guy, seldom seen without a dusty cowboy hat. He used to be a farm laborer—now he says he spends most of his time fishing.

Not exactly, as it turns out. He's into everything and everyone knows him. It was Duckworth who spearheaded a drive to stock a sawmill pond with rainbow trout so kids would have a place to fish. He sinks the profits from the tackle shop into gear and projects for the kids. He's served on the Paisley City Council and the school board. He teaches fishing at the school and he has his own hour-and-a-half radio show six days a week that's broadcast from the school. His reward in life, he says, is seeing kids walk through town on their way to the fish pond. His fear is that school attendance will drop below state standards, and students will be bused to Lakeview. No more school means no more school sporting events, no more graduations, and the end of an institution that ties the town together. It also would mean an end to a multiculturalism rare in Northwest towns, big or small.

During the school year, the town's two-story dormitory houses foreign exchange students brought from countries all over the world—Thailand, Ecuador, Mongolia, Japan, Kazakhstan are some. They boost the school's enrollment and bring a world perspective to a little town in the Oregon outback.

99

At the same time, the little town teaches them something about community and connectedness. Most are from cities with populations in the millions; Paisley's population is two hundred and fifty. These are kids who in one man's words have never seen a cow. By all accounts they come to love the place.

The dorm allows students and scholars of all stripes to stop over in Paisley for research projects or field trips, and they bring their own take on the world. Consider Paisley on a late Saturday afternoon during a recent Mosquito Festival. Buckaroos, as they call them in southeastern Oregon, and buckaroos in training packed the Pioneer Saloon, washing away rodeo dust with copious slugs of beer. At its most raucous, this may still have been a quiet evening for the Pioneer. It has been a bar for at least a century with time out for Prohibition. Country-western music hummed beneath the din, but somewhere outside in the warm early-evening air was another sound: the sliding whine of a guitar and snatches of what sounded like Bob Dylan.

The sound came from an asphalt alley next to the dorm. The dorm manager, Lance Richardson (who also builds log homes), sat before a pedal steel guitar and his son Andrew hit a set of electronic drums. They had teamed for a jam session with visiting Oregon State University students Cole Enabnit singing and playing guitar and Peter Little, also on guitar. They jammed for three or four hours with heart, soul, skill, and sophistication, never having played together as a group.

Travelers buzzing through town would hardly have known Paisley was there that evening, let alone the dorm, let alone Larry Duckworth, let alone the rodeo, the barbecue and the buckaroos in Pioneer Saloon. Cole Enabnit's husky voice putting out Dylan's "Knockin' on Heaven's Door" wouldn't have penetrated the climate-controlled bubble of an automobile.

The Basics: The Sage Rooms is a well-kept place in the heart of the action in Paisley. About twenty-five miles to the north is the Lodge at Summer Lake. The Homestead Restaurant in Paisley is open for breakfast, lunch, and dinner. The Pioneer Saloon is a classic friendly western watering hole.

Lakeview
2,700

The Road: One way to reach Lakeview is to travel north from
Bend on U.S. 97 and then cut off on Oregon 31 just north of
La Pine. Two of Oregon's most stunning geologic formations
appear on the way. Fort Rock, about forty miles from La Pine, is
an immense ring of compacted volcanic ash. Farther on is Abert
Rim, a steep cliff formed by a fault that extends thirty miles
and towers twenty-five hundred feet above the valley. Or for
an adventure, begin by traveling south from Burns on Oregon
205. The road dips into Nevada and passes through the parched
Nevada border town of Denio. Continue on Nevada 140 and
then Oregon 140. It's one hundred and seventeen miles from
Denio to Lakeview, over mountain passes that may require
chains in winter. From any of these summits, the views of rock
and sand valleys are solemnly magnificent. The terrain turns to
high desert and then to pine forests of the Warner Mountains.

Early on a clear day in Lakeview near the southern edge of Oregon, rise just as the sun appears over the Warner Mountains and drive east on Center Street into Bullard Canyon, green and gold in the filtered morning light. Continue to a sign that points to the hang-gliding launch and begin the winding drive up Black Cap Mountain. There's room to park near the top. Expect to stay awhile; the view is one of the most breathtaking in the Northwest.

The Goose Lake Valley spreads to the horizon, flat as a tight-pulled sheet in shades of gold and light salmon. To the south is Goose Lake, an alkaline body on the Oregon-California border. For hang gliders, the top of Black Cap is a superb place to launch into the sky. Winds over the valley pass across Lakeview, where they are warmed by roofs and asphalt and swiftly rise. A crease in the mountain funnels the air to the top, where it provides the updraft needed to lift hang gliders skyward.

They call Lakeview the hang-gliding capital of the West now and the sport brings tourists and new residents to town who wouldn't give it a second look otherwise. Take Mark Webber, a chunky, tanned emigrant from San Diego who came to sail the winds and now leads hang-gliding excursions.

"I'm kind of famous," he admits without conceit. He owns two dogs that follow him everywhere. One is pure white, and on special occasions, he sprays her with the appropriate soluble vegetable dyes. On St. Patrick's Day, the dog turns green, and on the Fourth of July, she is red, white, and blue. Residents, he believes, don't get the joke.

They may get the joke, but painted dogs aren't in their tradition. Irish farmers and sheepherders began arriving in Goose Lake Valley in the late 1860s, and Lakeview became a regional center. A fire in 1900 destroyed seventy-five businesses, but they were rebuilt in wood, stone, and brick. The nearest town of any size is Klamath Falls, one hundred miles to the west, but Lakeview doesn't feel isolated. The downtown's dignified buildings suggest a tradition of wealth and broad horizons, and the high education level here also may add to Lakeview's confidence. A fund established in 1922 by a wealthy physician, Bernard Daly, has provided college scholarships to hundreds of local students.

103

Besides hang gliding and a red, white, and blue dog, visitors to Lakeview and vicinity can experience Hart Mountain Antelope Refuge and also the summit of Drake Peak, which is said to overlook four states. But the sight in Lakeview that draws me back has nothing to do with views and geysers. I would even say it is one of the most moving and evocative artifacts in Oregon.

Dalpheus and Lula Schminck lived in Lakeview at the turn of the nineteenth century in a Sears, Roebuck Co. mail-order bungalow on Main Street. Over nearly sixty years of marriage, the couple assembled an impressive collection of pioneer artifacts, including porcelains, vintage clothing, hand-sewn quilts, silver, Indian artifacts, pressed glass, toys, gold watches, and much else. In 1936, they opened a small museum in their basement and, when Lula Schminck died in 1962, the house and its contents were left to the Oregon State Society of the Daughters of the American Revolution, which has maintained it as the Schminck Memorial Museum.

Framed in a dim hallway of the cottage museum is a child's beaded bag, scarred by a crudely cut oval hole and weighted with the history of the nineteenth century and one of the most profound population movements in American history. The bag belonged to Elizabeth Currier, who migrated from Missouri to Oregon in 1846 with her brother and sister, and her sister's husband. She was fourteen at the time and carried a beaded bag that must have been a treasure for an orphaned girl in a wagon train. The party took the Applegate Trail, turning at Fort Hall and proceeding southwest and then north over the harsh, alkaline Black Rock desert. They had just emerged from the desert when a seven-year-old child consumed a bottle of laudanum, a powerful opiate, and died. The family buried their child in the desert, and the resourceful Elizabeth cut a beaded flower from her precious bag and placed it on the child's grave. Elizabeth and her family settled in Benton County. Elizabeth married James Foster, and their daughter, Lula, later moved to Lakeview, where she married Dalpheus Schminck.

And so this little beaded bag in a little frame in a little hallway in a little house in a little town encapsulates in its way the essence of the Oregon Trail—pain, toil, grief, grit, determination, and the yearning for a distant Eden. Like the town of Lakeview and dozens of small towns in the Northwest, Elizabeth's bag is a hidden treasure.

The Basics: There are several good motels and restaurants in Lakeview at different price ranges.

105

Eastern Oregon

Eastern Oregon

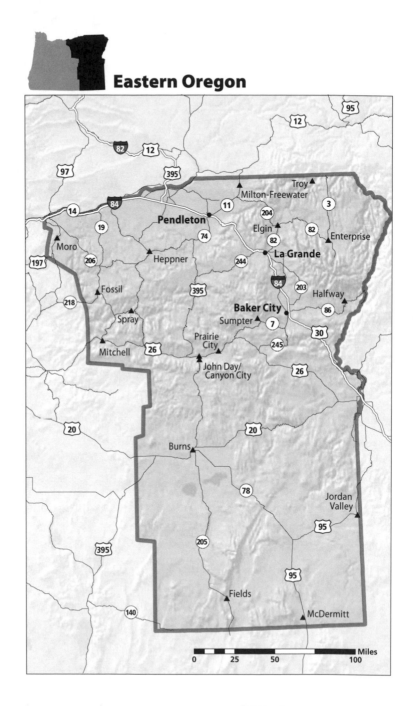

Moro
385

Moro from a distance is a patch of green in a sea of wheat. It's one of a string of Sherman County wheat towns, including Kent, Grass Valley, Wasco, and Rufus, all spaced about nine miles apart, the distance of a comfortable wagon ride. With a population of about eighteen hundred, Sherman County is the second-least populous in the state, but ranks third from the top in wheat production. The soft white wheat grown here is mostly exported and used for flatbreads, cakes, and ramen noodles.

Moro's Main Street is a break in U.S. 97, and big trucks rumble through all day. But the most persistent sound, particularly in the spring and summer, is the wind rushing through the poplar, locust, and cottonwood trees that offer welcome shade in this wide-open environment. Only 385 people live in Moro, but it feels like a larger place. It may be the grain economy that connects it to a bigger world, and it could also be the culture created by families that have lived here for generations, some in turn-of-the-century houses in town or on the farms.

Pioneers crossed Sherman County in waves beginning in 1843, fording the John Day River and then laboring up the steep, rocky hill to the Columbia Plateau. None of the early pioneers stayed behind, but a backsplash of immigration began in the late 1870s when farmers and stockmen came to the county. A general store was built in what is now Moro

109

in about 1879. The name Moro, after a town in Illinois, was drawn from a hat.

An emphatic sign of the local pride in history is the Sherman County Historical Museum, which was built and is run by volunteers. In 1994, it received the American Association for State and Local History's prestigious Corey Award for a volunteer-operated museum that displays "vigor, scholarship and imagination." About a hundred people volunteer at the museum, a large percentage considering the county's population. If a lucky cause in Multnomah County could achieve the same percentage for some kind of volunteer work, it would be swamped by forty thousand people.

The obvious pride that residents feel for the town doesn't necessarily extend to the downtown, which looks worn and neglected, the result of the changing agricultural economy, which means fewer farms to purchase fewer machines and bags of feed. Still, in this little town on the Oregon prairie, there's evidence of an arts scene. The Harvest Moon is a cooperative gallery that sells the work of local painters and sculptors, and across the street Lisa Shafer runs a quilt shop, Lisa's in Stitches. Shafer moved to town in 2001 when her husband was transferred by the Army Corps of Engineers to John Day Dam on the Columbia River. Seeking a way to fill her time, she opened a quilt shop, assuming that, in this out of the way place, it would occupy only a few hours a day. She hadn't figured on word of mouth, on the traffic on U.S. 97 or on the Internet, and the part-time diversion blossomed into a seven-day-a-week job. Now she makes quilts of her own and uses her long-arm quilting machine to quilt works that her clients have already sewn—about twenty-one hundred quilts at last count. She also teaches classes in quilting and sells quilting fabrics and supplies. Her Web site attracts clients from all over the world.

110

A successful visit to Moro means getting away from it. Early in the morning, particularly in late spring or early summer, jump on a bike or take the car out Van Gilder Road past the courthouse and turn left on Gordon Ridge Road. The ridge, a couple of miles ahead, offers sweeping views to the north of the checkerboard fields and purple hills of the Columbia Plateau. Wasco lies in a green blanket in the distance, and set in the landscape like exclamation marks are the towering white wind machines, which appear at every place where there's a breeze to catch. There are hundreds of them in Sherman County, and for the best views, take Old Wasco-Heppner Highway east out of Wasco to Klondike Road. Many resent their invasion, but the grace and presence of these monoliths, poking up out of the prairie, cannot be denied.

The Basics: The Tall Winds Motel is newly remodeled, nicely maintained, and well equipped. It's not a bad idea to make a reservation, because word about the place has spread. If nightlife is important, you can do better than Moro. At this writing, there is but one bar-restaurant, the Sweetwater Bar & Grill. You can also drive nine miles to Wasco, where the Lean-To Café & Goosepit Saloon serves daily specials including prime rib Saturday night, which is said to be the best in the area. The bar is a jolly place, patronized, it appears, by guys who work on the wind farms.

111

Fossil

465

The Road: The straightest route to Fossil is Oregon 19 south from Interstate 84 at Arlington. It passes through rolling wheat terrain, mostly deserted but for the town of Condon, which is the county seat of Gilliam County. The grim vicissitudes of agriculture are well told along the way by the wrecks of houses and barns collapsing in the fields. A rancher named Thomas Hoover gets credit for naming the town of Fossil in 1876 after fossils were discovered on his ranch. The fossils are part of the vast John Day Fossil Beds, a deposit that spans some forty million years and is one of the most complete records of ancient life in the world. For a small fee, fossils can be dug from a hillside behind Wheeler High School.

A rancher named Thomas Hoover gets credit for naming the town of Fossil in 1876 after fossils were discovered on his ranch. The love for things ancient apparently has persisted in the community. For a small fee, fossils can be dug from a hillside behind Wheeler High School. Also, the town's iconic emblem is a three-ton, fourteen-foot-tall woolly mammoth crafted of steel and bronze by Oregon sculptor Dixie Jewett. The work has acquired a patina that the artist describes as "good old Oregon rust," and each month it appears more rooted in the town and the earth. Fossil hasn't yet been able to scrape up the $60,000 purchase price, although a local group is working on it. Meanwhile, it stands on loan outside the Bridge Creek Flora Inn on Main Street.

The town huddles in mounds of softly rounded hills covered in sagebrush and juniper. The downtown on two intersecting streets includes a bar, a Chevrolet dealership, a bank branch, and a general store. It is an austere place of neutral colors and plain, straight lines. Most buildings sit close to the ground, with the exception of the Wheeler County Courthouse, built of red brick in 1901 and still towering over the scene.

For more reasons than fossils, this is a place where the past hasn't passed. The views of hills and big sky are the same as they were when Mr. Hoover arrived. In the early mornings deer amble down Main Street to snack on grass and shrubs. People still do their daily shopping in Fossil Mercantile, in business since 1883 and one of the few remaining general stores in Oregon. It sells food, fabrics, tools, candles, school supplies, handmade quilts, and virtually anything else that a reasonable person needs in daily life. Around the corner is the Fossil Museum, which displays a nice collection of artifacts from the town's history. First Baptist Church sits on a hill up the street from the museum.

The church with its commanding steeple was built in 1891, which means that it has seen ten thousand or so Sunday services. The pastor gives a heartfelt and engaging sermon, and the congregation sings stalwart Protestant hymns. It can't be that much different than it was a century ago and outsiders are welcomed warmly, probably as they were in 1891.

113

Apart from its buildings and setting, Fossil shelters a way of life that many fear is gone or sorely threatened. It is close-knit, hospitable, proud of its past and its culture. The town's institutions include a high school and grade school, a library, two museums, a motel, a general store, a full-service car dealership, a bed-and-breakfast set in two rambling houses, and a six-hole golf course. It has five churches by last count, numerous clubs, and a theater group, the Fossil Players. This is in a town of about four hundred and sixty people with no industry to speak of. It's three hours to Portland, an hour and a half to The Dalles, and two hours to Bend. Every summer, locals celebrate their home with a bluegrass festival, the county fair, a rodeo, and Mule Days.

Arriving in town, it's best to stop first at the Big Timber Family Restaurant for lunch or coffee and read the *Wheeler County News*. People come in to pass the time of day, among them members of the Red Hat Society, a group of women fifty and over who meet to hash out local affairs in which they are all involved. Voluntarism is big in Fossil; the town couldn't run without it.

And consider the Fossil Players. On one spring evening, the players presented Noel Coward's *Blithe Spirit* in the Wheeler High School gymnasium. Fossil Players was organized in the 1990s, and fifteen or so members compose the troupe. They present a melodrama every year during the Fourth of July Bluegrass Festival and a straight play or musical every year or two. Admission to *Blithe Spirit* was twelve dollars and that included dinner. First produced in London in 1941, the drawing-room comedy concerns a dotty medium, Madame Arcati, and the problems that arise when she visits the home of a married couple and conjures up the spirit of the husband's deceased wife. The cast included a city official, two school teachers, and a counselor. Who knows where they acquired their authority, their light comedic touch, their subtlety, their wackiness. The audience stood and applauded when the curtain fell.

114

The best way to end that evening was a drink at The Shamrock, a little bar-restaurant downtown. It's the only bar in Wheeler County (although this could change) and a regional institution well known to those who travel Oregon. Inside, its most noticeable feature is the walls, which are covered with scrawled messages, drawings, descriptions of memorable nights, and anything else that beer and good times may inspire. The practice of writing graffiti on the walls of the bar rather than the men's room began on Memorial Day weekend 1997. Owner Terry Ignowski had just painted the walls before taking off for an out-of-town trip. Returning a few days later, she found the walls had become a communal blackboard. Today she says ruefully, "It's yucky, but there are some things it's just better not fighting."

The Basics: The Bridge Creek Flora Inn and Fossil Lodge are two historic houses that compose a comfortable, atmospheric B&B. The Fossil Motel offers plain, reasonably priced rooms. The Shamrock serves food and drink in a convivial, graffiti-scrawled setting, and the Big Timber Family Restaurant also serves meals throughout the day.

115

Heppner
1,415

The Road: The most direct route to Heppner from Portland is to take Interstate 84 to Heppner Junction and travel southeast on Oregon 74. On the way, the town of Cecil is worth a stop for the Cecil store and for the associations here with the Oregon Trail. Farther on before reaching Heppner are the communities of Ione and Lexington.

Heppner is a place of tumbleweeds, towering grain elevators, and wheat fields. Solid, conservative brick and stone buildings line its broad Main Street and suggest sober pioneer values.

Architecturally, the town would be uninteresting if it were not for the Morrow County Courthouse, which sits grandly on a hill overlooking town. It was built in 1903 of locally quarried basalt in the American Renaissance style. Its flourishes include a grand flight of stone steps that lead from the street to the front door; and a white cupola that houses a clock and a bell. County leaders wisely have avoided drastic alterations to the interior, which remains finely proportioned and ornamented. The accommodating staff will show visitors around if time permits.

Northwest small towns are defined by their environment, which is visible from everywhere, whether it is sagebrush desert, forest, water, or rock. Heppner's environment is the wheat field. Wheat surrounds it, rippling in the wind, turning green, yellow, or brown, depending on the season. If you like the minimalist beauty of a wheat field, this is a lovely place. If the mechanics of wheat production are of interest, the Morrow County Agricultural Collection near downtown displays a thresher, a steam tractor, a windmill, and many other pieces.

116

Heppner got its start in 1869, when George Stansbury purchased land in the foothills of the Blue Mountains where five canyons converge, a setting that would haunt the town later. He and a partner, Henry Heppner, believed the site would become a crossroads, and they built a store on today's Main Street. The new town thrived as a center of wool, wheat, cattle, and timber.

The town's face and soul changed permanently on a burning hot day, June 14, 1903. At 5:16 p.m., the courthouse clock stopped, possibly because of electrical charges in the air preceding a thunderstorm. A cloudburst fell on nearby hills and sent a torrent crashing toward Heppner. A debris dam held it back, but when it broke, a wall of water inundated the town. More than two hundred people died—about a quarter of the town's population—and about a third of the town was torn apart. The flood lingers in Heppner's consciousness more than a century later, although construction of Willow Creek dam, which looms above a ball field on the edge of town, means that it probably won't happen again.

The flood is only one example of a pioneer past that Heppner mourns and celebrates. The Oregon Trail crossed Morrow County, and ruts cut by wagons, creaking, gouging, and swaying, are visible along the old trail, which is identified now by white markers. Maps available at the Morrow County Museum and in some shops downtown give fairly detailed directions on how to find the trail. The Willow Creek Crossing near Cecil, twenty miles north of Heppner, was a major rest stop for immigrants before they made their last push to the Columbia River. In Cecil just off the road stands a jaunty little red two-story building. It's the Cecil store, built in 1862 to serve local farmers and the last of the immigrants. It closed—or retired—in 1974, but like a wiry old farmer, it looks ready to go back to work at any time.

117

Jump ahead a few decades and visit Hardman, one of Oregon's most atmospheric ghost towns. It is twenty-three miles south of Heppner on Oregon 207. Settled in the 1870s, it and nearby locations went by several names, including Yaller Dog, Yellar Dog, Dog Town, Raw Dog, and Dairyville until a post office was established in the early 1880s and the more proper name of Hardman was conferred. The town thrived as a stage and freighting stop until the railroad came to Heppner. It sinks into the desert now, weathered and desolate, but it hasn't entirely dried up. An ancient building on the main road has been converted to a community center to serve the remaining twenty or so residents.

Little towns on the prairie don't fare well in a time of foreign competition, mechanization, and corporate farming, and Heppner is no exception, but its spirit remains. The annual St. Patrick's Day celebration draws spirited crowds to celebrate Heppner's Irish heritage, and spirit overflows at school sporting events. On winter nights, the town picks up and heads for a basketball game in Heppner High School or in a neighboring town. Sounds of cheering and rubber slapping on wood echo across the wheat fields.

The Basics: The Northwest Motel is clean, comfortable, and reasonably priced. The biggest challenge for a visitor is finding places to eat, especially at night. If you are not into bar food, bowling-alley food, or pizza, you may have to resort to supermarket frozen dinners and the motel microwave. The Willow Creek Diner is a good place for breakfast.

Spray
160

The Road: The easy way to Spray from Portland is to take
Interstate 84 to Arlington and then turn south on Oregon 19.
More of an adventure is to take U.S. 26 east through Madras,
Prineville, and Mitchell. About eight miles past Mitchell, look
for Waterman Road on the left (it later turns into Parrish Creek
Road). It is twenty-seven miles from here to Spray, and the road
is mostly dirt, but it's well maintained and passes through some
pretty country that not everyone sees.

Spray, a place named for a man and not a splash of water, lies in
a valley dotted with irrigated fields and groves of pine, poplar,
and locust. The John Day River flows past it, shimmery and
shallow, making a curve that wraps the town's edge. This is
rimrock country, and the underlying rock of the surrounding
hills is revealed in rust-colored bands that turn burnished gold
in the early morning and late afternoon sun. The town isn't
prettied up much because the setting lends all the variety and
beauty it needs. Oregon 19 connects it to other small towns,
including Service Creek, Fossil, Condon, and Arlington, but
it's still a jaunt to reach another outpost.

The town got its name from John Spray, who came in 1900
and helped establish a post office, then a ferry, and then laid
out the town. Two sawmills once provided an economic spine,
but those are long gone. The Spray Pioneer Museum is in a
recycled Baptist Church and includes a variety of artifacts
from the town's past, which doesn't seem that far behind it,
since Spray is definitely a place that recalls another era—let's
say seventy-five years ago at least. Elderly men gather on
the porch of the general store and exchange memories and

119

observations. Lots of the town's older citizens lived on ranches for years or kicked around the Northwest and they eventually settled here or "moved into town." The general tenor is polite and friendly. Everyone knows everybody else and a good many are related. About eighty students attend Spray schools, and elders speak of the young with affectionate approval. Spray has little serious crime, and small wonder because it's hard for anyone to go unnoticed. "You do anything and people talk about it," says Judy Simmons, manager of the River Bend Motel.

Newcomers aren't exactly pouring into Spray—the population has stayed at one hundred and sixty for several years. The people who do move here, or to Mitchell or John Day, are mostly retirees or people with a vivid independent stripe. An example of the latter is Bruce Gray who came to town in 2006 and opened a gunsmithing business, Grayguns, two miles outside town. He's a master gunsmith and grand master practical shooting competitor who brings a Zen perspective to the discipline. His company specializes in firearms instruction, industry consulting services, and high-grade pistolsmithing. He'll take your M1911 pistol or SIGARMS P-Series—or whatever handgun you own—and customize it just the way you like it. He also instructs in practical shooting, a term for shooting quickly and accurately at multiple targets. In his spare time, he serves as a Wheeler County Deputy Sheriff. He welcomes visitors to his shop but asks that you call first.

120

For a visitor, Spray is probably most hospitable in the late spring and summer when the river is low enough to be safe and high enough to speed a raft downstream. J & Z Shuttles serves boaters and rafters and will deliver your car to your destination. Rafts can be rented twelve miles away in Service Creek, which also offers shuttle service on the river. And if this sounds like too much work, there are several places to pull up for a swim or some fishing.

Neither of the town's two restaurants offer high cuisine, but the service is good natured and the food satisfies. The Lone Elk Café is in the back of the grocery store downtown. The River Bend Bar and Grill is up the street and serves daily lunch and dinner specials including prime rib on Friday and Saturday nights. The night sky serves as after-dinner entertainment. Without a strong artificial light source for miles, it is spangled blackness, quiet except for the river's silvery rush and the wind in the poplars.

The Basics: The River Bend Motel offers units in the downtown area and a two-bedroom house with deck near the river.

Mitchell

170

The Road: Crossing the Cascade Range from the west on U.S. 26, forested mountains melt away to high desert country. At Prineville, continue on U.S. 26 forty-seven miles through desert and over the Ochoco Mountains to Mitchell. And from Mitchell, it's seventy miles to John Day, meaning that it is a long way to the nearest little town in any direction.

You can speed past Mitchell if you don't know it's there. A huge tilted rock, the neck of an old volcano, announces that it's about a mile ahead. A road loops off U.S. 26 and curves into the town, which occupies a narrow canyon. It can't be much changed since the nineteenth century, when wagons loaded with goods stopped there on the way to the gold-rush town of Canyon City. The first structure was a blacksmith shop built in 1873. The location has been Mitchell's undoing several times. Flash floods roaring down the canyon tore it apart in 1884, 1904, and 1956.

Downtown is an intriguingly ragged collection of buildings, some fronted in weathered barnwood. There's also a gas station and a nice park on Bridge Creek. The best choice for accommodations is the Oregon Hotel, a two-story hostelry of a size rare for such a small town. It is the third generation of hotels built at that location, beginning in the nineteenth century. Fire destroyed the first two, and the current building was erected in 1938.

On warm days when the poplars whisper in the wind, visitors and townspeople gather on the hotel's hospitable front porch to observe Main Street's changing scene and exchange observations and gossip. Down the street, Patty Irby works behind the counter of Wheeler County Trading Co., a well-stocked general store. She's new in town.

"We love it here, but it's very ingrown," she says.

At night, stars gleam in the black sky and small sounds echo in the canyon. In an isolated village of one hundred and seventy, talk, tales, and gossip echo and reverberate too. It's hard to know how much to believe.

A bearded man talks bitterly of prejudice and unfairness that he claims have dogged him since moving to the area. Part of his lower lip was bitten off in a fight. He keeps it frozen in a jar. On a summer morning, a man at the gas pumps across the street from the hotel erupts furiously, claiming that a local businessman has slandered him. The blast of his anger is a blowtorch in the crisp, clean air. A while later, a man who lives in a tent outside town approaches. "The devil is a raging lion," he says. "He's seeking who he will devour."

In a town of echoes, it helps to have a strong relationship. Take Hugh Reed and Henry. Reed, a burly two-hundred-and-fifty-pound man, owns the town's only gasoline pumps and also the hotel. Henry is also big and burly but tops out at six hundred. Reed acquired the de-clawed black bear from a local boys' school that found him as a cub. He built a sizable pen for the animal behind his fuel pumps. Typical Henry breakfast is ten pounds of carrots, ten apples, and two gallons of dog food. Reed hugs and fondles the animal like a supersized teddy bear and on occasion wrestles with him. Once Henry tried to drag Reed into his lodge so they could hibernate together.

Another relationship that endures is Leonard Kopcinski and his wife, Cindy Vining. About forty years separate them; geology drew them together. From childhood, Cindy loved rocks. Kopcinsky, or Kop as he is called, has owned the Lucky

Strike Claim in the Ochoco Mountains west of Mitchell off U.S. 26, since 1953. Lean and tough as a stick, Kop admits he is lucky to have found a "one hell of a good woman."

The mine produces thundereggs—globes about the size of baseballs that reveal intricate patterns when sliced in half and polished. The eggs roll out of the dirt when it's loosened and Kop charges visitors a dollar a pound to excavate on their own. Sensitive as any artist, Kop adjusts the .44 magnum at his side, and leans forward intently to describe the varieties of thundereggs that he polishes himself. He becomes more eloquent about the Blue Mountain picture jasper that he mines at another claim. Cut and polished, picture jasper forms exquisite patterns that can be taken for a frog, a fish, a goose, or a tomahawk.

There are no echoes at Lucky Strike Mine, only the wind in the trees, the sound of thundereggs cracking together, and Kop's voice describing beauty in the rock waiting to emerge.

The Basics: The Oregon Hotel is the best place to experience Mitchell. There's also a lodge with three rooms next door above the Little Pine Cafe. The café is open for breakfast, lunch, and dinner, and if this fails, a glass of wine and a frozen dinner purchased at the Trading Company and microwaved in the hotel lobby can create a delightful evening when consumed on the front porch on a warm night.

John Day
1,850
Canyon City
670

The Road: Eastern Oregon is criss-crossed by a web of roads that makes most places easy to reach. The best routes into John Day are either on Oregon 19, passing through Condon and Fossil, or on U.S. 26 through Prineville, Mitchell, and Dayville. Either offers magnificent scenery.

The finest way for a newcomer to experience John Day is to drive to the top of Airport Hill at dawn. Below, the town awakens and golden light floods the John Day Valley. It is a lovely sight, and allows instant understanding of the reason people come here and stay.

John Day and its sister, Canyon City, sit in the middle of a vast patch of Eastern Oregon territory. It's 266 miles east of Portland, 145 miles east of Bend, seventy miles north of Burns, eighty-two miles from Baker City, and there's not much in between.

Gold was discovered on Whiskey Flat near Canyon Creek in 1862. Standing in Canyon City's silent downtown, the tumult of the gold-rush days can barely be imagined. Chinese laborers thronged to the area to work in the gold fields. Saloons, brothels, blacksmiths, and churches sprang up. In 1870 a fire destroyed much of the early town, including the first courthouse, and in 1885 Canyon City's Chinatown burned to the ground. The Civil War came to Canyon City on July 4, 1863, when Union sympathizers stormed Rebel Hill and tore down a flag raised by Confederates.

You can place yourself in old and new Grant County by attending a service at St. Thomas Episcopal Church in Canyon City. It is a narrow, wooden Gothic Revival structure with steeply pitched roofs, window frames that point to heaven, and finished inside in knotty pine. Built in 1876, it survived three major fires that swept the downtown. The presence of a spring that still bubbles up next to the church may have saved it.

On a Sunday morning, the congregation follows about the same ritual and sings the same hymns that their forebears did in the 1870s. Little Oregon congregations usually can't support their own pastor, and in Canyon City they rely on priests who rotate in from other churches. Among these circuit riders is Ivor Hughes, a witty, avuncular priest from Yeoville in Somerset, England, who with his wife is spending five years as an interim priest in Klamath Falls.

"Vast and nothing like England," he says of his American home.

Hughes prays and asks for special concerns from the congregation. A woman offers prayers for "the calves in the fields." In the early spring in John Day and environs, it is not overseas wars that occupy people's minds—it's the little creatures asleep in the meadows that represent the future. After the service, the congregation troops next door to the church hall for potluck lunch, a kind of frontier tradition to which first-timers and old-timers are invited.

If St. Thomas Church looks solid, the surrounding communities are shaky. The timber harvest from the Malheur National Forest is a fraction of what it used to be, meaning fewer sawmills and fewer jobs, and the county population is ebbing slowly. Canyon City can rely on its position as the county seat, and John Day remains a commercial center to some degree and a traveler's stop. Main Street John Day doesn't deteriorate but it doesn't pretty-up much either. It remains a quietly nostalgic small-town business district with drugstore, hardware, and a bank. Traffic through town ensures that the motels will hang on, and there are several restaurants, which suggests some disposable income.

There are many ways to enjoy the riches, cultural and scenic, of the area: float the John Day River, visit the Sheep Rock Unit of the John Day Fossil Beds National Monument (on Oregon 19 between Dayville and Kimberly), fish, hunt, drive, bike, and ride horseback. Closer to home is the Grant County Historical Museum in Canyon City, located near where gold was discovered in 1862. In addition to the usual artifacts of pioneer life, it includes the Joaquin Miller cabin, a structure dating from the 1860s. Miller was a poet who achieved some nineteenth-century renown as the Poet of the Sierras. Nearby is the 1910 Greenhorn Jail, a two-cell calaboose kidnapped in 1963 from its original location in the gold-rush settlement of Greenhorn. A few blocks from the museum is Oxbow Trade Company, an unusual business that features an extensive collection of wagons and buggies.

But John Day's most singular attraction is the Kam Wah Chung Museum, rare, wonderful, and even today, a mysterious place. It was built as a trading post on the Dalles Military Road in about 1866. In 1887, Chinese immigrants Ing Hay and Lung On bought the building. Lung On was an entrepreneur and Ing Hay an herbalist and master in pulse diagnosis. Their business served as grocery, Buddhist temple, doctor's office, and opium den. They jammed shelves with exotic Chinese and typically American goods: candy, cigarettes, ginseng, gambling supplies, and dozens of other items. Doc Hay also oversaw an apothecary collection: bear claw, dried lizard, fawn skeleton, a bottle of rattlesnakes, in addition to hundreds of medicinal herbs. One room contains two sets of bunk beds. The walls

127

and ceiling are blackened, it appears, from opium smoke. Doc Hay went to a nursing home in 1948, and his heir later donated the building and its contents to the city. It was closed and locked until the 1970s when local volunteers removed the contents, cleaned the building, and replaced every item exactly as it had been found. The museum's future is secure after a $1.5 million restoration completed in 2007. It's a true time capsule.

The Basics: The Best Western John Day Inn on Main Street is a comfortable place to stay. The Dreamers Lodge a block off Main Street also is clean, comfortable, and a good value. There are a couple of steakhouses in town as well as Mexican restaurants, and one Chinese restaurant located in Canyon City.

Prairie City

1,100

The Road: One way to get to Prairie City and have a good time on the way is to take the Journey Through Time scenic byway, which starts at Biggs Junction, east of The Dalles, and continues to Baker City, on the edge of Oregon. On the way, it passes through Moro, Shaniko, Fossil, Spray, Dayville, and John Day, often following the John Day River. Pamphlets that describe the byway are available in most tourist centers and the route can also be found on the Web.

On a stormy day in Prairie City, clouds pile above Strawberry Mountain and vertical prongs of lightning hit the ground like Jupiter's thunderbolts. Front Street's muscular stone buildings stand square-shouldered against the elements like loggers and miners, refusing to be moved, and the weather heightens the town's isolation in the Upper John Day Valley.

Prairie City's population has hung in at around eleven hundred for years. Agriculture, cattle, and timber once paid the bills, but timber is flaking away and people hack out a living, sometimes jumping between several jobs. They stay on because it's a beautiful place to live, surrounded by soaring mountains and a lush, well-watered valley.

The town's origins date from 1862, when a group of Confederate sympathizers camped along a stream now called Dixie Creek and discovered gold. A town called Dixie sprang up, and when the gold petered out, people migrated three and a half miles to the present site of Prairie City. In 1865, a military outpost, Camp Logan, was established by the First Oregon Volunteers five miles south of Prairie City on Strawberry Creek with the mission of protecting the Dalles Military Road. When

129

the war ended, Union Army officers were sent out to replace the volunteer officers. The fort closed in 1869, and although there is no evidence that any of the Union soldiers remained in the John Day Valley, the presence of these seasoned veterans, with stories to tell of the terrible war, must have had an impact on the town.

Nadia Schultz, who is assistant curator of Prairie City's DeWitt Museum, has identified twenty-eight graves of Civil War veterans in the old Prairie Cemetery, and she believes there are more. Traces of the war still appear like gold flecks in a mountain stream. In 2004, Amy and Warren Giandomenico moved to Prairie City from Portland and opened an antiques shop in a stone building on Front Street. Amy was surprised by the items she kept turning up in the little town and surrounding ranches: a Civil War saber, furniture and clothing from the 1860s, a plumed Civil War hat, an 1860s quilt. It's not much of a stretch to assume that some of these remnants of the 1860s were brought to the area by soldiers, miners, and farmers who had traveled west seeking a new start after the war. They carried with them a few treasured possessions—perhaps a saber, a plumed hat, or a quilt. As ranchers clean out attics and barns, more of these remains of a nation recovering from the wounds of war may turn up.

For years, Prairie City lived in isolation in a valley that fills with snow in the winter, but it isn't socially isolated anymore. Hunters, hikers, and alpine skiers pour through town and they have two lodging choices now, the Strawberry Mountain Inn, a bed-and-breakfast based in a commodious house built in 1906, and Hotel Prairie, a nine-room hostelry on Front Street. The hotel opened in 2008 after extensive remodeling of a 1905 building that served as a hotel until the late 1970s. Most downtown businesses keep an eye on tourists but remain rooted in the town. The name of the Oxbow Coffee House and

130

Restaurant (formerly the Shoshoni Winds) clearly borrows from twenty-first-century trends, but the building has been a center of Prairie City commerce since 1902 as an auto repair shop, a butcher, and later a restaurant.

Rosewood figures and carvings ornamenting the bar were crafted in Milan, Italy, and shipped to St. Louis, Missouri, where the bar was built, and then shipped to Portland around Cape Horn in 1879. From there, it was hauled by sternwheeler to The Dalles, by train to Baker City, and by wagon to Prairie City, where it was installed in the building now occupied by the Bank of Eastern Oregon. It was moved to the present building in 1959.

The restaurant also features a cliché of western-themed restaurants: stuffed animal heads. It's hard to find a table in the long, narrow room that's not accessorized by a dismembered beast hanging above. The heads may not be the right stimulant for squeamish appetites, but anyone interested in the biggest and best in taxidermy and Northwest game animals should have dinner with them.

The heads, which are on loan, come from some of the largest animals ever taken in the Northwest. These include record whitetail deer, elk, antelope, mountain goats, and an Alaskan moose with a seventy-two-inch antler spread (the twenty-seventh largest moose ever taken). At this writing, they are on tour, however, and it's possible they will not return.

131

Nightlife in Prairie City? It depends on the season. In this town and most small towns that still function as communities, the center of public life is the school, and to get a feel for the town, or just a rousing good time, you can't do better than attend a school sporting event. The Prairie City High School athletes play football, volleyball, basketball, and sometimes baseball, and run track. At this writing, the lights aren't functioning on the football field, and games are played in the afternoon, but that will change. A night ball game in this town—the smell of trampled grass, the cheers, the sharp chill—will stick in memory longer than any movie, and the same goes for a basketball game.

"It's still the best show in town," says Prairie City School District Superintendent David Kerr.

The Basics: The Strawberry Mountain Inn is a warm, roomy B&B, and Hotel Prairie has been carefully restored and given a beautiful period feel.

Sumpter

170

The Road: The most efficient way to get to Sumpter is to take Interstate 84 east from Portland three hundred miles to Baker City, and then Oregon 7 west toward Sumpter. More scenic is to take I-84 to Pendleton and turn south on U.S. 395 to Ukiah and continue southeast on U.S. Forest Service roads through Granite to Sumpter, but these Forest Service roads may be closed in the winter.

Sumpter, before all else, is a gold town, the center of one of Oregon's richest strikes. That's mostly history now, but Sumpter retains a rugged, independent spirit characteristic of gold-rush towns. Slouched along the main street is a collection of buildings, some dating from the late nineteenth century, but this is hardly a replacement for the town's original business district—eleven blocks of it—which burned to the ground in 1917. Large-scale mining dried up here in the 1950s, but a few miners still hack at the rocky soil and insist there are riches to be found. The town depends on tourists now, drawn by the gold dredge and the Sumpter Valley Railroad. The locals are friendly, not too much changed perhaps from the hard-working, fun-loving miners.

Gold was discovered in the vicinity in 1862 by five southerners who named the cabin they built Fort Sumter after the place in Charleston Harbor, South Carolina, where the first engagement of the Civil War took place in 1861. The town's name was later spelled as Sumpter. Gold exploration continued in three waves of technology: first placer mining, then hydraulic, and finally hard rock. The town memorializes its mining, logging, and ranching history in the Sumpter Municipal Museum, located in an 1899 mercantile building

133

on Mill Street. Among its artifacts is a small collection of possessions left behind by Chinese miners, who flocked to the place. There's a barrel that once held soy sauce, an old leather shoe that even today seems exotic, and also a collection of tiny wooden carvings recalling the old country. It is a moving record of what must have been a lonesome effort by a homesick carver to recall his home.

On the edge of town in a little pond sits a massive wooden contraption, looking something like a derelict three-story boarding house. It weighs twelve hundred tons, and its size becomes all the more impressive when it's considered that it moved, and that it and two predecessors cranked and growled through the Sumpter Valley, digging a swath six and a half miles long and a mile wide. This is the Sumpter Valley Dredge, a mighty machine for extracting gold. A moving line attached to the structure was fitted with seventy-two iron buckets, each weighing a ton, which gouged deep and brought up earth that was washed and sent through a rotating trommel fitted with a screen that separated rocks from gold-bearing sand.

Sumpter people have wheels in their heads. They like to move around and they like their machines. For recreation, the wheels come in two sizes: little rubber rollers attached to all-terrain vehicles and the big steel wheels that carry steam locomotives. The Sumpter Valley Railway runs locomotives on weekends and holidays between Sumpter and McEwen, about five miles apart. The original narrow-gauge railroad operated from 1890 until 1947, when it was scrapped, but volunteers recreated the railroad, hauling track, ties, and spikes and acquiring the locomotives. It takes about an hour each way to make the trip and although it's a fun way to step back in time, it couldn't very well be called scenic. On all sides are gravel hills, melancholy reminders of the days when the dredges shoveled through what once was a lovely valley. You can

134

push deeper into the country if you bring along a snowmobile or an all-terrain vehicle. The surrounding Blue and Elkhorn mountains are crisscrossed with some three hundred and fifty miles of groomed trails that lead into green forests and to views of deep valleys. Trail maps are available around town, and for a more personal viewpoint, stop by Borello's and talk to bartender Carl Swinyer. He says he doesn't lead tours, but he doesn't mind if you follow him.

There are a couple of restaurants in Sumpter, among them Borello's, which is well known locally for its Italian fare, particularly the pastas. Ron and Cheryl Borello came to Sumpter in 1969 and bought a little restaurant to which they later attached a bar. The restaurant's recipes had been passed down in Ron Borello's family, which emigrated from northern Italy. Cheryl Borello works the kitchen, preparing the pastas and lasagna from scratch. The restaurant spills over into the bar most nights, making this a convivial place to eat, drink, and converse. Harvey Halvorsen stops in regularly. In 1982, he retired from a U.S. government job and started a new career with his wife as a gold miner, which he continued for twenty-six years. He'll tell you all you want to know about gold mining, and appall you with stories of a recent burglary at his house that cost him about $40,000 worth of gold and silver. Once a gold town, always a gold town.

135

The Basics: For a town its size, Sumpter offers a range of accommodations, including the Sumpter Bed and Breakfast and several cabins for rent. There is also the Depot Inn, a tidy fourteen-unit motel. The Elkhorn Saloon & Restaurant offers forty-two variations on the hamburger, and Borello's across the street serves its Italian specialties, on Friday, Saturday, and Sunday nights. The Scoop-n-Steamer Station Café, housed in a log structure, serves good breakfasts.

Milton-Freewater

6,500

The Road: Milton-Freewater is reached on Oregon 11, through Walla Walla, coming from the north, or from the south through Pendleton. This is wheat country, broad and rolling until the fields meet furrowed mountains marked by swaths of charcoal-green trees that crawl up the draws.

Milton-Freewater is a gritty blue-collar town, scratched from the dirt in the 1870s. Well-worn, unpretentious buildings line the main streets. An exception is the Milton-Freewater Public Library, completed in 2004, which is all wood and glass and looks like a two-story Craftsman-style lantern. The town has most things that one this size requires and some besides. There's a Safeway, a drive-in movie theater open April to October, and several restaurants and motels. Prosperity in Walla Walla just five miles away doesn't seem to trickle south, however.

The town's peculiar name is the result of a temperance squabble. When the town of Milton was incorporated, the sale of liquor was not allowed. Later a group of thirsty citizens founded the adjacent town of Freewater, named for a promise that free water would be provided to all home sites. The towns merged in 1950 as Milton-Freewater.

Locals mock their town affectionately—Muddy Frogwater, they call it. For years, Milton-Freewater celebrated itself with a summer pea festival, but when pea production declined, the town reinvented the event as the Muddy Frogwater Festival. It's held the third weekend in August and draws thousands to hear blues and country music. Jumping up all over town—over fifty at last count—are man-size frog statues, personalized to reflect their owners: judge frogs, chiropractor frogs, bookworm frogs, skateboarding frogs. Muddy-Frogwater, they say, is "A Toadly Awesome Place to Live," and the pun potential is limited only by the species.

The finest way to spend a Muddy-Frogwater morning is to leave it and drive thirteen miles to Harris County Park in the foothills of the Blue Mountains. The road follows the South Fork of the Walla Walla River and ends at a trailhead that continues farther into the canyon. This is a lovely drive at any time of year, even in winter when the hills above the gushing river are black, brown, mottled green, and yellow.

Instead of returning to Milton-Freewater, backtrack on Oregon 11 to Weston, secluded off the main highway in rolling wheat fields. Downtown Weston is a picturesque collection of one-story nineteenth-century brick buildings. The Long Branch Cafe and Saloon on Main Street, built in about 1874, is a good place for breakfast and, judging from the group in the bar at 10 a.m., for an early morning snort.

Although Weston looks like a place where the winds of change don't blow at gale force, it still has industry to support its seven hundred or so residents. Smith Frozen Foods, which processes peas, carrots, corn, and lima beans, employs eight hundred people at peak season. Regular tours for the public aren't offered—a missed opportunity. More people would enjoy seeing mountains of peas flash frozen than the company might imagine.

More accessible is the local apple industry. Walla Walla Valley apples are some of the finest in the world, juicy, crisp, and delectably sweet. In the fall, LeFore Orchards in Milton-Freewater sells big boxes of Braeburn, Fuji, Gala, and Delicious apples at a fraction of what they would cost in the store. And not far from the LeFore outlet is the Blue Mountain Cider Company tasting room, where crisp, bubbly hard apple cider can be tasted and purchased.

137

Still, one of the most moving experiences in Milton-Freewater has nothing to do with apples, cider, or five-foot frogs. It is a house with a story attached that shines a light into a tragedy that occurred over a century ago.

William S. and Rachel Paulina Frazier came to the Walla Walla Valley in 1867. They purchased land and in 1892 built a commodious house that passed to their descendants. The house and furnishings were willed to a local foundation and opened as the Frazier Farmstead Museum in 1984. Among its treasures is a cache of Civil War letters found in a tin box in the bottom of a trunk, and a bullet taken from the arm of one John Warren, who was caught in the act of robbing the post office. Dr. C. W. Thomas treated the miscreant in 1897.

You could easily overlook a photograph on the home's second-floor landing of little Claude Frazier (known as Claudie), nearly four years old, and his sister, Zelma, taken in 1895. Shortly after the photograph was taken, Claudie slipped while playing on his rocking horse and fell into the fireplace. He died twenty-four hours later.

You will find Claudie's grave in the Old Pioneer Cemetery, which is up a steep dirt road near a communications tower. I could provide directions to the grave, but it's best to stroll among the markers and find it yourself. Claudie's stone has been tumbled from its base into the dirt, a piece of banged-up marble like many others in the desecrated cemetery. Doubtless, the grave was tended lovingly for years.

This is the inscription: "Claudie died Nov. 24, 1895 3 years 8 months 24 days. He is at rest in heaven."

In the early evening, lights blink and flicker below, and beyond the town, the Walla Walla Valley stretches to the Blue Mountains. Claudie enjoys a splendid view.

138

The Basics: The Morgan Inn is a comfortable place to stay. There are several restaurants in town, including a Mexican and a Chinese.

Troy
13

The Road: There are said to be six roads in and five roads out of Troy, although some are rocky and rough. The most comfortable route begins in Enterprise. Take Oregon 3 to Boggan's Oasis, a café, and then continue northwest for eighteen miles on Grande Ronde Road to Troy.

The most remote place in Oregon? There's Jordan Valley in the far southeast corner of the state, McDermitt, a hamlet on the Nevada border, and Powers, high in the Coast Range. Add to the list Troy, a few miles from the Washington border on Oregon's northeast edge. Apart from its setting, the town itself might not seem worth the effort it takes to get there. It is a place of trees, dirt streets, and a few modest houses set in a valley beneath canyon walls. The thirteen or so people who live here, however, might believe they're in heaven if they fish, raft, hike, or just enjoy the sound of silence. The Wenaha and Grande Ronde rivers converge here and the river canyons that cut through rust-colored rock are among the loveliest in Oregon. Also, Troy is on the edge of the Wenaha-Tucannon Wilderness, a place of forests and deep canyons prime for horseback riding and hiking its two hundred miles of trails.

Troy hasn't always been a little town near the vanishing point in the middle of nowhere. Once it was a bigger place in the middle of nowhere. Mormon settlers arrived there in 1898 and called the place Nauvoo, after the town in Illinois from which Mormons were expelled in 1846. The town became a small regional center with a hotel, a sawmill, and a three-story grist mill. But the sawmill and grist mill closed and the highway bridge that once crossed the Grand Ronde River at

140

Troy was moved two miles upstream, and traffic bypassed the place. Meanwhile, investors have bought up some of the nearby ranches, which means fewer jobs for local people if the new owners don't operate working spreads.

It comes as a surprise, even a shock, to arrive in town and see a sign that announces a Shilo Inn. Shilo is one of the Northwest's largest hotel chains with forty big hotel/motels in ten states, so why, you might ask, did it choose to expand into the Troy market? The answer lies with one person, Mark Hemstreet, the owner of Shilo Inns. Hemstreet owns a ranch in the mountains above Troy, and about twenty-five years ago, he bought an existing lodge complex, which includes a café with three hotel rooms upstairs, three cabins, a twenty-space riverside RV park, a campsite for tents, and another building with showers and laundry. He leases the place now, most recently to Doug Mallory, who grew up in the area, and it is now the Shilo Troy Resort. If the Shilo is full or closed, another place for a bed and a meal is Boggan's Oasis, about eighteen miles down Grand Ronde Road from Troy.

The proprietors of Boggan's Oasis, Bill and Farrel Vail, preside over a dying breed of roadside hospitality: the roadside diner. Their restaurant sits on Washington 129, the 141 continuation of Oregon 3, just four miles from the Washington border at a place where the Grande Ronde River makes a hairpin curve. Inside, it is an oasis of sociability and good food in a setting that otherwise offers few refinements and almost no competition. Customers drift in and out all day, arriving by car, bike, truck and motorcycle. The only other restaurant in the vicinity, provided it's open, is at Troy. Otherwise, for a burger, a shake, or a plate of chicken-fried steak, you would have to drive forty miles north to Clarkston or about forty-five miles south to Enterprise.

Farrel Vail didn't plan to become a cook—she calculates this is her third or fourth career preceded by stints as a florist and a professional ice skater at Sun Valley, Idaho. She dishes up steaks, salmon, pork chops, and burgers, but judging from the traffic, it's the milkshakes, ice cream, and freshly baked pies that pull in most of the trade. Over breakfast one morning, I watched three pairs of motorcyclists arrive, and all ordered pie, pie a la mode or ice cream cones. Boggan's also sets up boat trips over the length of the Grande Ronde River, most often for anglers fishing for rainbow and Dolly Varden trout, whitefish, squaw fish, suckers, bass, and steelhead. They also rent RV spaces and three small but comfortable cabins with little decks that are nice places to sit back and feel night descend on the river canyon.

The Basics: It's not a bad idea to call in advance and reserve a room if you intend to stay overnight in Troy or at Boggan's Oasis.

142

Enterprise
1,940

The Road: There are a couple of ways to get to Enterprise, but the most efficient is to take Interstate 84 to La Grande and continue northeast on Oregon 82. The road is a proper overture to the town, winding along the Wallowa River past valleys and aged barns that are the essence of the western mountain landscape.

Ask people why they live in Enterprise, an isolated town in the northeast corner of Oregon, and a common response is "Can't you see?" or something like it. It may have the most beautiful setting of any town in Oregon. The Wallowa Mountains rise gloriously before it, dwarfing the little town and its fine old stone buildings. In winter, the mountains are brilliantly white and clouds rise and fall around them like theater curtains. In summer, they stand charcoal green against a clear blue sky.

White settlers arrived in the Wallowa Valley in about 1872 and the town was incorporated in 1887. Local merchants determined to make it the most prominent in Eastern Oregon and successfully promoted it as the county seat. They constructed their buildings of Bowlby stone, named for a man who owned a nearby quarry, and today they remain solid and dignified.

143

Town leaders debated what to call the new town, and one suggested that whatever they chose, the place was bound to be enterprising. They quickly settled on Enterprise. A walk in the downtown suggests that enterprise, if flagging, remains. There's a pharmacy, a clothing store, and a good bookstore. Anchoring it all is the sturdy 1909 Wallowa County Courthouse.

It is a place that welcomes newcomers—or at least accepts them once they show that they will be around for a while. Fewer people work in the woods now, but there's been a big increase in non-profit organizations, such as Fishtrap, which hosts workshops and conferences for writers and students in a bungalow near the downtown.

With a population of about two thousand people two hundred miles from a city of any size, residents create their own entertainment. For starters, they read. The Bookloft has occupied the same spot on Main Street since the 1970s. They also keep an eye on events. On a fall weekend, locals pondered choices. Half the town seemed to have been invited to a blowout sixtieth birthday party Saturday night in nearby Joseph. Also, they could attend a square dance in the Hurricane Grange hall, a high-school play in Joseph, and a benefit dinner at the Elks Lodge in Enterprise.

This is not to say that Enterprise is socially and politically homogenous. Consider the clientele of the Terminal Gravity brewpub and of the Range Rider tavern. The brewpub is housed in a bungalow on an obscure lane at the edge of town. In the summer, patrons sip and socialize on the lawn beneath an alder grove and in the winter they stick inside at the bar or huddle on the front porch. Behind the bar you might encounter Yasha Sturgill, whose white hair is cut above a face of chiseled beauty. She wears a diamond nose pin and an all-black outfit, and as her style and bearing would suggest, she is a trained dancer. She still teaches dance in Enterprise, where she moved in the early 1990s after long involvement in the arts and politics in Portland.

Terminal Gravity's patrons are photographers, artisans of many stripes, aging hippies, Forest Service employees, and backpackers. I've never seen what appeared to be a rancher or a truck driver, although I'm sure they have been spotted.

A pair of brewers, Dean Duquette and Steve Carper, founded the brewery in 1997 and deliberately chose this out of the way neighborhood in an out of the way town.

An aged neon sign announces the Range Rider tavern in the downtown. It's a cheery western saloon where people come to eat good, simple food and have a few drinks. It opens at 6 a.m. and the cook is up early, frying eggs and bacon and making gallons of coffee to serve to leathery ranchers and blue-collar guys who tease, banter, and discuss the price of whatever.

Energized by eggs, hashbrowns, and too much coffee, the best thing to do in Enterprise in the morning is head for the hills. The lanes leading out of town are irresistible for driving and biking. Near the foot of the mountains in a metal barn on Sunrise Road, Erl McLaughlin, a barley farmer, maintains a museum of antique tractors and steam equipment. He displays thirty or more antique tractors including a 1915 Case Tractor that looks like it was designed blindfolded. There's also a 1908 portable steam engine and various other machines, all of them rescued from rust and rot.

In another direction just off Oregon 3 (Enterprise-Lewiston Highway) is the Stangel Buffalo Ranch, where you can stop and view these great, rheumy beasts in their corrals. Thirty-seven miles farther is the nearly deserted town of Flora, once an agricultural center. A handful of people remain, including Vanessa and Dan Thompson who run a bed-and-breakfast, North End Crossing Barn & Bed, in this isolated spot and also head a foundation dedicated to restoring the nine-thousand-square-foot, two-story Flora School, vacant since 1977.

And then there's Joseph, just up the road from Enterprise. Once a mill town, it reinvented itself in the 1980s as an art center where bronze sculpture is cast in three local foundries. It's not the Old West, for sure, despite the false fronts and many authentic buildings. Over the years, it has eclipsed Enterprise,

145

which pokes along as the seat of county government. Enterprise has better views and fewer restaurants, more residents and not as many tourists on the streets, a more authentic western feel and less of what is called charm. The towns are close enough, however, that both can be enjoyed.

> *The Basics:* There are several good motels in Enterprise. The Ponderosa is attractive and well maintained and it's located downtown. Chinese and Mexican food compose the international fare here, and good food is also served at the Terminal Gravity brewpub and at the Rough Rider bar.

Elgin

1,700

The Road: From Portland, it is an easy three hundred miles on Interstate 84 provided snows haven't closed the mountain passes east of Pendleton. Take the first exit into La Grande and continue on Oregon 82.

Elgin in northeastern Oregon is a place of old stories, old buildings, and old-timers. One old story concerns a cowboy who came to town to see a shoot-'em-up western movie at the opera house and became so engrossed that, at a climactic moment, he got to his feet and opened fire on the screen. The town's surroundings in the Grande Ronde Valley are solemnly beautiful, all the more so in winter when fields are beige, the Blue Mountains white, and forests a somber charcoal green. The town still has the feel of a late-nineteenth-century outpost of civilized society and architecture. Looking north on Main Street are several stalwart stone buildings that were built, it appears, to hold the line between civilization and the forested mountains beyond.

Native Americans were already gathering in the vicinity to catch and smoke fish when the first white settlers arrived around 1865. A telling artifact of early days is the 1897 city jail, which sits near the Opera House and offers a grim example of the wages of sin at the time. When the railroad arrived in 1890, Elgin became a trade and supply crossroads for north Union County and much of Wallowa County. The newly prosperous residents built fine homes of native stone and local brick in Gothic Revival, Greek Revival, Italianate, and Queen Anne styles. Now most of the buildings are peeling and chipping away; businesses that cater to real people's needs, as apart from antiques shops, are scarce, and many of

147

the people you meet are sadly resigned to the town's continued decline. This may or may not happen. People still come to town and stay, drawn by the beautiful surroundings and the sense of community.

A spark plug in Elgin for the last couple of years has been a young impresario named Terry Hale who came to town in 2006 and organized Friends of the Opera House. Hale already had directed community theater in Oregon City and Canby, but it's not clear where he got the daring to lease the Opera House and mobilize local talent to present serious musical theater. For his first production, he took a leap and produced Disney's "Beauty and the Beast," a musical with a cast and crew of over one hundred. It was a big success.

By leasing the Elgin Opera House, Hale acquired a fine example of a turn-of-the-twentieth-century small-town American performance hall. Completed in 1912, it was embellished with a pressed-tin ceiling, ornate molding, and box seats on each side of the stage. A restoration was carried out in the late 1980s and improvements continue. Plans are underway now to move the Elgin Museum & Historical Society, which now shares the building, to new quarters and turn the entire Opera House into a performance center for music, dance, and drama. Another museum, one that moves, is Eagle Cap Excursion Train, which operates on a sixty-three-mile line that connects Elgin in Union County with Enterprise and Joseph in Wallowa County, following the Grande Ronde and Wallowa rivers. The line, completed in 1908, was abandoned in 1997 and later taken over by Union and Wallowa counties. A variety of excursions are offered, including in February and March the Steelhead Train, which begins at Minim, about a twenty-minute drive from Elgin. The train crawls at about fifteen miles an hour, dropping anglers off at prized fishing holes on the Wallowa River, and ending at Rondowa, where the Wallowa and Grande Ronde rivers meet.

Occupying time at night might be a challenge in Elgin. Movies are shown at the Opera House on weekend nights, provided a musical show isn't being rehearsed or performed. The other alternative in fall and winter is a basketball or football game at Elgin High School. As in all small towns, the schools are the center of the community, and a brightly lighted school gymnasium, shaking with action and cheers, is the best place to be on a dark night.

Otherwise, you can always barhop. Americans don't barhop as much as they used to, but it makes more sense in Elgin because the town's three bars in about a one-block area are the centers of drinking and gastronomy. The Huang Cheng Restaurant and Lounge serves good Chinese food, including an excellent spicy chicken. The Brunswick Cafe and Lounge and Sig's Restaurant and Saloon across the street serve American food with an emphasis on steaks and prime rib. All three spots can be empty as Dracula's grave at night or they can jump with talk and pool—you take your chances.

And if you are lucky, you will be able to arrange to be in Elgin the last weekend in January or the first weekend in February when a rodeo club, the Elgin Stampeders, stages the yearly crab feed. The club travels all the way to Seaside on the coast and brings back one thousand pounds or so of freshly canned crab that they dish out, all you can eat, along with potato salad, baked beans, coleslaw, and French bread. And if you are really lucky, there will be basketball games at the high school starting in the afternoon and continuing into the evening.

In short, counting sporting events, the excursion train, and possibly a musical performance or a crab feed, little Elgin, which looks like it's sliding into ruin, will wear you out.

The Basics: Elgin's only motel, the Stampede Inn, has been steadily upgraded over the last few years. The rooms are spacious, clean, and brightly decorated and the price is right. It's best to reserve early for the few weekends when the town fills up. The Whitehorse Cafe on the south edge of town serves good breakfasts. On the way to Elgin, stop by Union County Tourism at 102 Elm Street in La Grande. Janet Dodson, the executive director, will load you down with useful maps and brochures, suggest things to do, people to talk to, and in general communicate her enthusiasm for the area.

Halfway

355

The Road: Halfway is fifty-five miles east of Baker City on Oregon 86. From June through November, the Wallowa Mountain Road, or Forest Road 39, connects Joseph with the Hells Canyon National Recreation Area and with Halfway. It's paved, but steep and winding.

Halfway lies in the Pine Valley on the edge of the Wallowa Mountains. Northeast is Hells Canyon, a chasm cut by the Snake River. Fifty-five miles in the other direction are Baker City and Flagstaff Hill, where pioneer immigrants first glimpsed Baker Valley and the Blue Mountains.

It's a droll place, and that can't be said of many little western towns. The steeple on Pine Valley Presbyterian Church is painted bright watermelon. The town bed-and-breakfast is a fantasy of carved creatures and shapes attached to weathered buildings. The underlying exuberance of Halfway received national attention in 2000 when an e-commerce company, Half.com, approached the town with a publicity scheme to change its name for a year to Half.com in exchange for money, computers, and other offerings. The company erected a sign on the road into town announcing "America's First Dot-com City"—this for a town of 355 people that looks like cattle could be driven down Main Street. The publicity, it's said, was worth millions for Half.com (the company), which was later bought by eBay.

People in Halfway make their living on ranching, tourism, and whatever else might turn up. Many who leave drift back, drawn by the mountain views, crisp, clear air, and the sense of a place removed from twenty-first-century life. More

151

than many small towns in the Northwest renowned for their quality of life, Halfway has combined new people and new points of view without losing its cow town flavor. On one side of Main Street, Babette Beatty sells her brilliantly colored impressionist-style paintings. On the other side, Tami's Pine Valley Funeral Home displays photographs and affectionate obituaries of recently deceased citizens of the valley.

Dale and Babette Beatty may have seen the church steeple as an encouraging sign when they came to the valley in 1992. He was a builder and woodworker with a flair for fanciful designs. She was an internationally known German-born model who had taken up painting. They remodeled several ramshackle Main Street buildings, including an empty church, embellished them with Dale Beatty's imaginative flights in wood, and created Pine Valley Lodge. The Beattys have since sold the lodge to local ranchers, but it will always bear their stamp. Dale has moved on but Babette remains, painting and selling from the old church building.

You can spend a good day in Halfway just hanging out: have breakfast at the Stockmen's or at Wild Bill's Cafe and Bar, take a look at the Pine Valley Community Museum, and if the road is clear of snow, perhaps drive to the ghost town of Cornucopia in the mountains north of Halfway, the site of one of Oregon's richest gold strikes.

It's a good idea to buy a copy of the *Hells Canyon Journal* and keep an eye on fliers posted in the taverns. These inform of local events—perhaps a lecture at the library or a high-school basketball game. And for a jolly immersion in regional culture, the best time to visit is the second Saturday in March when Halfway Lions Club holds its annual crab feed. The Lions Club began this unlikely venture in 1967 as a moneymaker to support a scholarship program, a food bank, and various other civic projects. Crab feeds are not uncommon in Eastern

Oregon, even if the source of the main item on the menu is four hundred miles away.

A thousand or so show up for the event every year and consume nearly a ton of cracked Dungeness crab. The club and its volunteers also prepare two hundred and seventy loaves of garlic bread, a potato salad that contains three hundred and fifty pounds of potatoes and sixty dozen eggs, and untold amounts of baked beans, coleslaw, beer, and soft drinks. They start serving at noon, and the last guest doesn't depart until about 9 p.m. Experienced old-timers bring their own implements: nutcrackers to crack the crab, picks to remove it from the shell, and small chafing dishes set over candles to melt butter that they bring in squeeze bottles.

People line up outside, some coming from Idaho and points beyond. Many bring six-packs and twelve-packs to ward off the chill and are fairly warm when they get inside. The ratio of beer to soft drinks served changes, with beer far tipping the scale as the event wears on. It's figured that each person will consume about two pounds of crab.

"People who come to our crab feed are professional eaters," says Ralph Smead, an organizer of the event.

The crab feed is an exuberant exclamation mark in the town, a lot like the watermelon steeple. 153

The Basics: The Pine Valley Lodge is the place to stay in Halfway. It's comfortable, homey, and pleasantly offbeat. But the Halfway Motel is a reasonably priced, conventional alternative, particularly the rooms in the newer addition. Wild Bill's Cafe and Bar and the Stockmen's serve good café food. Be forewarned: tickets to the crab feed are not available at the door. They can be ordered in advance from Ralph Smead in Halfway or from the Halfway Lions Club.

Jordan Valley

230

The Road: The fastest way to reach Jordan Valley from the Portland area is to take U.S. 84 east all the way to Ontario and then U.S. 95 south. The more scenic route is to cut across the center of the state, passing through Bend and Burns, and then head southeast into the Oregon outback.

Jordan Valley sits along Jordan Creek in the far southeast corner of Oregon. The business district is two gas stations, two motels, two bars, and a hardware store, and almost all the buildings look like they could be hauled away in a day or two. It's a place of rock and sagebrush that blend in striking combinations. Sweeping valleys end in bluish mountains and dirt roads lead to pockets of rock columns, arches, and spires in shades of reddish gold and yellow. The sky can be pale blue hung with shredded clouds.

It may sound like an end-of-the-road cow town but Jordan Valley has more legend, lore, history, and ethnic diversity than places hundreds of times its size. The richness of its culture is found in the taste of a Picon Punch, a visit to a nearby gravesite, and in the origins of the name of the Owyhee River, which flows through the desert here and gives its name to Owyhee Country.

A Picon Punch at the Old Basque Inn is a good way to get acquainted with the place provided driving is over for the day. A Basque specialty, the drink combines Picon liqueur, grenadine, and soda with a float of brandy on top top— bittersweet and delicious.

White settlers arrived in Jordan Valley in the early 1860s when gold was discovered at Jordan Creek. Cattle arrived soon afterward and became the mainstay of the local economy. Basques began settling here in 1889, working as sheepherders, stonemasons, and hotelkeepers. Near the Old Basque Inn is an L-shaped stone wall, built in 1915 by Basque stonemasons as a *pelota frontone*, or handball court. It was restored in 1997, but local Basque descendants seldom use it, nor, it appears, do the locals consume much Picon Punch. The bartender who made my drink had to consult a recipe.

Intriguing bits of ethnicity are scattered throughout the territory and not confined to Basques. The Owyhee River was named for a party of three Hawaiians—Owyhee is an early spelling of Hawaii—who set out to explore the region in 1819. One was found murdered in camp and the rest were never heard from again. And consider Father Elias Munyaneza. Father Munyaneza, a Roman Catholic priest with the Apostles of Jesus, ministers to congregations in Jordan Valley as well as Nyssa and nearby Arock. He speaks in the lilting accents of his home in Uganda. He came to Oregon in 2003 after completing studies for the priesthood in Nairobi, Kenya. He loves the Jordan Valley despite its isolation and cowboy roots. "I am not an American or a white, but I have been accepted by the people," he says.

Adventurers are drawn to this corner of the state—it may be its isolation or its broad, arid vistas. Or more likely they come because that's where the opportunity is. One of America's most famous adventurers died here in 1866. He was an old man, passing through on horseback. His death was noted and quickly forgotten, but tales circulated for years that a famous "half-breed" was buried at Inskip Station, a ruined hostel about seventeen miles from Jordan Valley. It wasn't until the 1960s that the rumors were confirmed by discovery of newspaper accounts from 1866 that reported the death of Jean Baptiste Charbonneau, who was the youngest member of the Lewis and Clark Expedition.

Charbonneau was born in 1805 at Fort Mandan, North Dakota, the son of a French trapper, Toussaint Charbonneau, and a Shoshone woman, Sacajawea. The child traveled on his mother's back to the Pacific Ocean and back. William Clark nicknamed the boy Pomp or Pompy for his attitude of pomp as he danced around the party's campsites, and Clark later became the boy's guardian. As a young man, Charbonneau, as a protégé of a European nobleman, traveled throughout Europe, learning German, French, and Spanish. He returned to the United States and headed again for the frontier, becoming a guide, magistrate, trapper, and miner. He was on his way to gold fields in Montana when he caught a chill crossing the Owyhee River and died of pneumonia.

The few accounts of his life, often in the journals of other travelers, portray a well-educated man, probably an anomaly among his peers. He lived most of his life and died on the American frontier, spanning race, culture, and time in a way few Americans ever have. Inskip Station is now a pile of stones. The Charbonneau grave is fenced by weathered wood. A tattered flag flies above it.

156 Owyhee country is a fine place to explore, particularly in a four-wheel-drive vehicle with sturdy tires. Exploration is easier if you pick up a little brochure folded lengthwise in quarters. Its title is *Welcome to Jordan Valley, Haven of the Best in the West*. Printed below is *Gure Etxea Zure Etxea*, a Basque phrase that means "Our house is your house." The brochure contains a surprising amount of information crammed into a small space, including history of the Basques, Jordan Valley history, a list of things do in the valley, and a large hand-drawn map that shows obscure destinations.

If that's not enough, the locals will happily answer questions. Waitresses in the JV Café and the Old Basque Inn treat travelers with warm concern; the men in the service station change a punctured tire and almost apologize that it happened. Directions are given freely and precisely, and always accompanied by solicitous advice. The guys in the JV saloon can be loud and boisterous but they would stop everything to jump a stranger's dead battery.

Gure Etxea Zure Etxea, indeed.

The Basics: For a town of only about two hundred and thirty residents, Jordan Valley is nicely provided for tourists. The Basque Station Motel is reasonably priced and comfortable and the Old Basque Inn serves good American-style food and some Basque specialties. The JV Cafe adjacent to the bar is a cheery place for a meal or a cup of coffee.

Burns

5,000

The Road: To reach Burns from Portland, go first to Bend, in Central Oregon. The highway commercial strip between Redmond and Bend is one of the ugliest in Oregon, but the scene changes a few miles outside Bend on U.S. 20. What unfolds is mostly a sagebrush plain, but the vistas are wide open and refreshing. Gritty roadside towns pop up along the way: Millican, Brothers, Riley. What's ahead is isolated western culture, more turned in on itself than Bend and Redmond and much more connected with a tough, venturesome past.

The road to Burns unwinds in a straight black line and it's tempting to step on the gas and aim for the bluish hills. That apparently was the state of mind of the Oregon pioneers— floorboard their lives and head for the horizon. Burns (and adjoining Hines) appear suddenly out of the desert. Physically, it's a sparse, grayish place that sits close to the ground. "I didn't feel culture shock, I felt horticulture shock," said one woman who relocated to Burns from the green Willamette Valley.

158

After almost a century and a half of settlement, the town still seems impermanent as if the next strong wind, physical or economic, could blow it away. Tenacious as sagebrush, it holds on. White settlers entered the Harney basin in about 1870 looking for land and water to support their cattle. A hotel was built in 1881 and saloons sprang up, among them Frank Lewis's Brewery Saloon, the Red Front, the Elite, and the Gem. The oldest commercial structure on Broadway is the Brown building, built of local stone in 1896. The autopsy of Peter French, the legendary nineteenth-century cattle baron, was conducted in an upstairs room of the building after a homesteader shot him in 1897. The upstairs also found use as a dance hall.

Burns hasn't changed much; it has evolved. The dance hall is long gone from the Brown building and a little deli serving hot soup and sandwiches occupies a first-floor space. In addition to the usual civic groups operating here, a chamber music society and a writers group bring culture to town. But the people Peter French saw on the streets in the 1890s are still around: women hunch against the wind pulling children along, men with hide gloves stuffed in back pockets slip into bars for a beer.

On a bitter, windy day, the Harney County Historical Museum is a warm refuge, and nearby, the library offers a place to absorb local history or check e-mail. But to understand Burns, you have to leave it. The High Desert Discovery Scenic Byway passes through the most dramatic and scenic attractions in this remote part of Oregon, including the Malheur National Wildlife Refuge, Steens Mountain, the Hart Mountain National Antelope Refuge, the Alvord Desert, and the Peter French Round Barn. The latter, as an insight into the mindset and determination that created Burns and still pervades the area, shouldn't be missed. French built it in about 1880 as a place to break in horses on his huge ranch during the winter. It's a round stone corral surrounded by a wood-enclosed outer-circle paddock for breaking horses. At the center, an umbrella-style truss supports the vast roof. 159

Horses remain at the center of Harney County life. The county is said to rank ninth in the United States in production of beef cattle and nearly half the county's taxes come from ranchers. It's a good idea to watch the local newspaper for adult and high-school rodeos at the Harney County Fairgrounds. The rodeo game for kids in Harney County is particularly complicated. The kids may be equal but they're not the same. There are rodeo kids and buckaroo kids, or flathats as they are sometimes called. Rodeo kids live in town and own horses. Buckaroo kids live on ranches. Riding horses, roping, and cutting are part of their daily lives. Buckaroo kids don't crease the crown of their hats—hence flathats. Flathats don't often participate in rodeos, probably because it sounds too much like work.

The Old West, where ranchers scrape out a living from the soil and don't see an outsider for weeks on end, is still the way of life in much of the county. Heading east from Burns, stop off in Crane, a flat jumble of a town where the most significant landmark is the white spire of a Mormon church. The Crane School District serves kids who live on ranches in the Oregon outback. Beginning at middle school, they live in the school dormitory and head back to the ranch on weekends. Proud parents still come in to see their boys and girls play football and volleyball. Then they transport them home, say seventy-five or a hundred years away.

The Basics: Lodging is plentiful in Burns. For meals, there are several steakhouses, a Mexican restaurant, and even one that serves Thai food. Shoppers usually head east twenty-three miles on U.S. 20 to Buchanan, a dusty outpost that looks like a gas stop but is the home of Oards Museum and Gift Shop, which offers a wide selection of Native American jewelry and crafts.

160

McDermitt
200

The Road: McDermitt, on the Oregon/Nevada state line, can be reached from several directions. One is to come from Winnemucca, Nevada, taking U.S. 95 into Oregon. From the north, it's best to go through Burns, continuing south on Oregon 78 and U.S. 95.

The way to McDermitt coming from the north or south is a strip of asphalt, unrolling in a black line through vistas of sagebrush and barren mountains colored blue and mauve. On hazy days when the dust whips up, the landscape is less distinct and the distant mountains are like wobbly cutouts at the edge of the world.

The town in the Quinn River Valley sits so low in the desert that you could be on it, through it, and speeding away before it registers. Straddling the Oregon/Nevada border, it has two motels, a gas station, three bars, and a little market. The big business is the Say When Casino, which stretches about half a city block along the road. For all its size, the casino is upstaged   161
by the ghostly White Horse Inn, which stands alone on the edge of town. Closed for nearly a quarter of a century, it looks like the decaying set of a Western film. The Clanton gang could ride up at any moment. The desert gently encroaches now, but recent efforts at restoration may push it back a bit.

First thing to do coming into town is stop at the Say When. After a few hours on a lonely desert road, it's an oasis of light and noise—slots tinkle and cheery lights blink. Order a Coke or a beer at the bar and chat with the bartenders, who usually know everyone in town.

McDermitt dates to 1865 when President Lincoln ordered construction of a fort at what is now the Fort McDermitt Indian Reservation. Col. Charles F. McDermitt took command but died in an Indian ambush west of town and the fort and later the town were named after him. The original name of the town was Dugout, after a store dug into the side of a hill.

Living on the line of two states as different as whisky and apple juice gives residents a casual attitude toward boundaries. They are there to be crossed. From the top of Buckskin Mountain, a few miles south of McDermitt, the states of Oregon, Nevada, and Idaho can be seen as a vast panorama of valleys and mountains. In this grand setting, belonging to just one state means less than being part of the whole.

Locals welcome visitors and, time permitting, they'll stop for coffee and talk about the place. Sometimes, they'll even show you around. George Wilkinson is a third-generation rancher and owner of Little Meadow Ranch. He lives on the Oregon side of the border but like most McDermitt people, he considers himself a Nevadan.

"This whole area is more or less known as Nevada," he says. "The majority make their home in Nevada and our language and politics is based around what is happening in Nevada."

Retired from day-to-day ranch operations, he remains as straight and lean as a wooden stake. From the top of Buckskin Mountain, he can point out his ranch, a green spot in the hazy distance. Beyond is Ten Mile Ranch, where his grandfather settled in 1879 with a dream of raising sheep and horses

"I spent my life pretty much on horseback since I was a little boy," he says.

For years, Wilkinson drove cattle every March for three and a half days from the Quinn River Valley to spring pastures near the three forks of the Owyhee River. Even today, buckaroos conduct the drive on horseback with only a four-wheel-drive pickup to carry supplies.

For a wide spot in the road, McDermitt has a social cohesion that bigger towns might envy. Everyone knows everyone else's foibles, strengths, and histories. Residents of Fort McDermitt Indian Reservation work in town and join in community activities. The tribe's administration buildings sit near the old fort's commissary, which now is a community center. Nearby, untended and gaping open, is a solitary stone structure that was the fort's jail. Inside, two cells with concrete floors and slatlike iron bars look like the proper place to reflect on misdeeds.

Ernestine Coble, a tribal member, shows visitors around. At the time of my visit, the valley was undergoing the worst drought in memory. Thirst-crazed cattle were jumping down into river canyons and couldn't be pulled out. Coble was perplexed when a couple of weeks earlier some visitors came to the reservation and performed a sun dance. "I said heck with the sun dance," she said. "We need a rain dance."

When the sun goes down, McDermitt settles into starry night, the quiet broken by trucks lumbering down the dark highway. It's about a thirty-second walk from the McDermitt Motel to the Say When for a steak. Afterward, McDermitt's options are limited—maybe a walk to the edge of town to stare out into the hushed desert or a stop by the Desert Inn, a little joint across the street from the Say When.

Illyssa Fogel owns the place. She was a bankruptcy lawyer in Los Angeles when she saw a newspaper ad for a fifteen-slot-machine bar for sale in McDermitt along with a motel, the Diamond A. She reckoned that there had to be a better life than traffic and sprawl, and when her offer was accepted, she lit out for McDermitt.

163

"This is a great place," she says of her new home. "The weather is wonderful. I don't miss L.A. I have high-speed access and Direct TV and what more do you need?"

The Basics: The McDermitt Motel and the Diamond A Motel provide clean, basic lodging. The café of the Say When Casino is good for breakfast, lunch, and dinner and for a snack if you're passing through.

Fields

13

The Road: *The Road:* Fields is in southeast Oregon, twenty-one miles from the Nevada state line. Anyone in the mood for a dirt-road adventure might consider taking Oregon 78 south from Burns, and then continuing south on U.S. 95 to Whitehorse Ranch Lane. Turn right there, and it's forty-nine miles on dirt to Oregon 205. Fields is a few miles north. On the way, you will pass the sixty-three-thousand-acre Whitehorse Ranch, established in 1869.

Once, before the interstate highway system cut a six-lane swath through the West, there were lots of places like Fields Station in the tiny settlement of Fields. On lonely desert roads, they meant a room for the traveler cooled by a roaring swamp cooler that pulled in hot dry air from the outside through water-soaked straw pads. Pies sweated behind glass at the lunch counter. Hamburgers were on the menu, as well as grilled-cheese sandwiches and BLTS served with ice water, Coke, or milkshakes. The roadside stop was an oasis, and not only for cool air and icy drinks; it was a place of safety, electric lights, and friendly conversation after hours spent in a hot car crossing a dirt and rock desert.

165

A modern automobile now could be several degrees cooler than the Fields Station Café, but the place, about twenty miles north of the Nevada/Oregon border, remains an oasis. The store is stocked with beer, soft drinks, and an odd variety of canned goods that come in handy if you are staying at the motel. Thick milkshakes are whipped up in a variety of flavors and the café offers a menu of burgers and sandwiches that are served to travelers on the way to Steens Mountain or to local ranchers. A condition of running a place like this, according to an ex-owner, is to never run out of ice cream, dog food, and chew.

In addition to the café and adjoining motel, post office, and gas station, the town includes a few houses and a thick grove of trees that's watered by Fields Creek. Owls and other birds rustle in the leaves and birdwatchers are said to value the place.

Fields dates from 1881, when it was established as a station on the stagecoach line between Winnemucca and Burns. A stone ruin on the edge of the trees was the original horse barn and some of the early settlers rest in a little graveyard behind the café. The population now is down to nine, but it doesn't seem in any immediate danger of shutting down since ranchers in the vicinity patronize the store and send their children to Fields Elementary, a K-8 institution with a student body of about fifteen.

Travelers who opt to stay in Fields overnight can choose between motel-style rooms or a freestanding three-bedroom wooden structure called "The Hotel." No TV, no radio. The café closes at 6 p.m. and by nightfall, the whole place is quiet as an empty ants' nest. The hotel has a microwave and, if you arrive before the store closes, you can buy a frozen dinner or a can of chili to eat on the darkening front porch with maybe a side of canned string beans and a cold beer.

As night sinks over the valley, the air sings, chirps, and mutters. A few rustlings are heard and then a few more— deer or rabbits perhaps or maybe something else. The silence amplifies every noise, and, in a night black as this, the front porch seems as wild and remote as the desert beyond. Owls flop silently around the ruined stable, and no doubt the little graveyard out back is alive with rattlesnakes. In the morning it's nice to take a stroll around town although you will encounter more jackrabbits than people. Then it's time to drop into the café for eggs, hashbrowns, and coffee. The place gleams in the sunlight—it's the other side of night.

Local society seems a lot like the desert, empty from a distance but buzzing with activity the closer you get. Young people here entertain themselves with speed and noise, pretty much as they do in Los Angeles. Racing cars on Alvord Desert, a sizable dry lake north of town, is an option, and a night's fun can be had by filling up a cooler with beer and shooting jackrabbits. Nearby hot springs offer warm dips for those not already overheated by the desert sun.

"It's a peaceful place," says Charlotte Northrup, a former Fields Station owner. "Living out here, we are a close community. It's a lot different than living closer to town. A lot of people come here, almost petrified because it's so far out and so quiet."

After a couple of days, she adds, they don't want to leave.

The Basics: The basics here are very basic, confined to Fields Station, a cheerful, welcoming place that sells some basic groceries and also operates a café, motel, and gas station.

167

Southern Washington

Southern Washington

South Bend

1,770

The Road: To reach South Bend from Oregon, cross the Columbia River at Astoria, where the river spills into the ocean. The Lewis and Clark Expedition was near the end of its westward cross-country journey here in November 1805 and spent six of its most uncomfortable days marooned on the northern shore by huge waves. The explorers called the place "the dismal nitch" and it's still there. It's best to continue on Washington 401 through Naselle, and then go north on U.S. 101 skirting the bay and forested hills.

On a rainy day on Willapa Bay, charcoal green trees prop up a droopy sky and the gray horizon brushes against gray-green water. You have to accept a gray-green world to live on Willapa Bay. You should also have a taste for oysters. Raw or fried, an oyster can make up for a lot of gray.

The superb Willapa Bay oyster owe its quality and numbers to the bay's clean, cold waters, which are flushed regularly with seawater allowing the plump bivalves to grow firm and clean. Oysters are the reason most people come here: to make money from them, learn about them, smell the sea in their glistening bodies, eat them raw or fried and enjoy their voluptuous flesh with their unctuous melding of firm and silky soft.

The bay is a pocket extending about twenty-five miles at the southwest edge of Washington. Little towns dot its edges, most of them based on oystering, fishing, and tourism: South Bend, Tokeland, Bay Center, Oysterville, Nahcotta. South Bend clusters on the Willapa River at the bay's edge. Weathered century-old buildings line its downtown street and up a hill, the Pacific County Courthouse, completed in 1911 in second

171

Renaissance Revival style, announces a time of past prosperity and exuberance. The building's design, grandiose for the time, earned it the title "the gilded palace of extravagance"—small wonder, considering its magnificent art-glass dome.

Trees, fish, and oysters have driven the town's economy with the exception of a remarkable interlude of land speculation in the late nineteenth century. There are stories of one Philander Swett, a roguish land speculator whose misadventures are documented in probate records preserved on microfilm in the county clerk's office.

For an immersion in oyster culture, take U.S. 101 south from South Bend and follow signs that point to Bay Center, a village at the edge of Goose Point Peninsula, a narrow finger of land that protrudes into the bay. Indians once camped and traded here. The first white settlers arrived in 1853 and generations of fishing people lie in the town's pioneer cemetery. Hillocks of bleached white oyster shells, the refuse of years of oystering, dot the town, and oystering remains a big business. A few oyster plants near the main road process oysters and sell oysters and fresh fish that are caught in the bay and unloaded in the little boat basin.

172

Dick Wilson, President of Bay Center Mariculture, farms oysters, shipping about a hundred thousand bushels a year that are sold mostly in the western United States by restaurants that serve them cooked or raw on plates of crushed ice and salt. He explains the life cycle of oysters, from the moment of conception when the water can turn milky from eggs and sperm, to the point where the larvae settle on shells and begin to grow their own shells. It takes two to four years for an oyster to mature. Oysters, he says, are a sustainable crop, grown and harvested in a way that not only doesn't pollute but actually cleans the water. They're also the perfect food, he explains, low in cholesterol, low in calories, high in important minerals. Listening to him, the Swedish author Isak Dinesen, who in old age subsisted on oysters and champagne, doesn't seem eccentric.

Just above the basin is Dock of the Bay, a little bar and restaurant that has offered warmth, solace, and oysters to generations of oyster gatherers. Inside, fisherfolk sit at the bar over morning coffee or late-afternoon beer. The owner, Ricki Bayne, presides like the proprietress of a Wild West saloon. She's warm and offhand and cooks up a plate of oysters that she serves with coleslaw, toast, and fries. Visitors can watch her in the galley. She pats the oysters dry and dredges them in seasoned flour. Then she lays them on a lightly oiled grill heated to about 350, ladles a little more oil around them, and cooks them until they are golden brown. Her deep-fried oysters for lunch are a treat and her grilled oysters for breakfast with eggs and hashbrowns will keep you happy the rest of the day.

The best weekend visit to Bay City and South Bend is unstructured and vagarious, enjoying the bay, the oysters, and the scenery. A place to end the day is the Chester Tavern, a tough-looking little waterside bar that serves food. In a bar like this in the city, the fare would be burgers, nachos, and microwaved poppers. Here it's oysters.

173

The Basics: The Seaquest Motel is comfortable and reasonably priced. Chens Motel on the east edge of town offers good basic rooms although it looks less than inviting from the road.

Ilwaco

1,070

The Road: Take U.S. 26 to the coast, then travel north on U.S. 101, through Astoria and across the Astoria-Megler Bridge. Continue on U.S. 101 to Ilwaco.

Ilwaco is a well-scuffed little town on the south end of Washington's Long Beach Peninsula that manages to keep its character while doubling as an important tourist destination. To the north, the narrow peninsula extends about thirty miles with the Pacific Ocean on one side and Willapa Bay on the other. An excursion on Washington 103 will cover its length, past the booming tourist carnival of Long Beach, and north to Nahcotta and Oysterville. The latter was a nineteenth-century boom town based on oysters harvested from the shallow bay beginning in 1854.

Water is all around, and the culture of water is everywhere—in the Ilwaco Marina, in the two lighthouses that beam warnings from the edge of Cape Disappointment State Park, in the oysters taken from the bay, the fish harvested from the ocean, and in the river that surges past the town.

Mornings in Ilwaco, big gruff fisherfolk shoulder into Don's Portside Café for breakfast, and the place hums with town gossip and friendly greetings. But the town also appeals to out-of-towners with several good places to stay, a couple of good restaurants where fish is on the menu, and a wine bar in the marina.

It's an unassuming place and barely hints at the drama and history of its setting where a great river meets the ocean. At least 234 ships have been stranded, sunk, or burned near the river's mouth. When the Lewis and Clark Expedition arrived

174

here in 1805, they discovered a thriving Chinook Native American population and a sizable village. The town has done full justice to its history with the Columbia Pacific Heritage Museum, where well-designed exhibits explain the Lewis and Clark Expedition and Native American culture and even provide a stirring account using text and video of the French adventurer, Gerard D'Aboville, who rowed a twenty-six-foot boat from Japan to Ilwaco in 1991.

The park is the place to begin and end a visit to Ilwaco. The Cape Disappointment loop road starts on the edge of town and leads into a forested enclave of winding trails, and some of the Northwest's most dramatic and historic views at the mouth of the Columbia River. All of the trails are magnificent, but if time is limited, choose the Discovery Trail, which cuts through the park, extending eight and a half miles from Ilwaco to Long Beach, following roughly the route that William Clark took on an exploratory hike up the peninsula coastline. Much of it is paved, and highlighted by dramatic works of art that commemorate the expedition. The Lewis and Clark Interpretive Center is also located in the park. And for anyone who relishes the life of forty-foot waves, helicopter rescues, and boats that can flip over and right themselves, the Cape Disappointment Coast Guard Station offers tours, time permitting.

And if the park is the jewel of the peninsula, it never hurts to have fun with an artificial gem. Marsh's Free Museum in Long Beach, a few miles from Ilwaco, is a schlock 'til you drop kind of place, packed with stuff for sale and hokum to disapprove of. The hokum is international class and includes Jake the Alligator Man, half-man, half-alligator, so they say, a creepy-looking thing that looks like it crawled out of a nightmare.

Also, for a more genteel experience, get to know Susan Wallace, who presides over Painted Lady Lavender Farm, about two miles outside town. The lavender farm genre in the Northwest can be fragrant at best and precious at worst. This one is endearingly eccentric, located on two densely designed and planted acres that include beds of lavender, little nooks, pens of chickens and quail, a profusion of blooming plants and vines, and Wallace herself. She and her husband, Dwight, created the place in the late 1970s. She sweeps through the property, digging, planting, building, and playing the saxophone, on which she is self taught. She decks herself out in extravagant jewelry and romantic floating finery rescued from a thrift shop—just the right attire for a lavender farm. It's open seven days a week from 10 a.m. until 7 p.m. except Sunday, when it closes at 4 p.m. Visitors are encouraged to bring lunches and picnic on the grounds.

At the end of the day, seek refuge at the Raven & Finch, a wine bar in a town that seems geared more to beer drinkers. It occupies a little structure in the marina, and since the owners haven't bothered much with signage, it takes a sharp eye to pick it out. Live music and impromptu jam sessions are featured, and in the summer, the little deck that looks out on the water is a fine place to sip and sun.

And if you are fortunate enough to be here in early May, head for the marina on Saturday morning for the blessing of the fleet. Boats carrying passengers without charge churn in a line to the mouth of the river where wreaths are dropped in memory of boaters and fisherfolk who have died in the last year in the surrounding waters. Water, as I said, defines the place.

The Basics: Tourists throng the peninsula in the summer and as a result there are lots of motels, bed-and-breakfasts, and restaurants to choose from in Ilwaco and on up the peninsula. The Inn at Harbour Village is a spacious bed-and-breakfast in a 1928 church. Heidi's Inn is cheaper, offering clean, spacious rooms in the downtown area. For meals, Don's Portside Café serves breakfast in a warm, small-town setting. The Imperial Schooner in the marina serves excellent oysters and fish and chips, while the Depot, the Pelicano, and the 42nd Street Café offer more upscale fare. A good first stop for maps, brochures, and helpful tips is the Long Beach Peninsula Visitors Bureau in Long Beach.

White Salmon

2,220

The Road: The most scenic route to White Salmon is to take Washington 14, which follows the Columbia River on the Washington side. At Bingen, take Washington 141 a mile and a half to White Salmon.

White Salmon sits on a bluff overlooking the Columbia River, and although it's only sixty-five miles from Portland and hardly isolated, the location makes it feel apart. You could zip by on Washington 14 and not know it's there, assuming that Bingen down on the riverfront is all there is. White Salmon's shopping district, which inhabits an aerie above the river, is surely the most splendidly scenic in the Northwest. Rising behind is the gently rounded Burdoin Mountain, matted with deep growths of oak and fir, and ahead soars the bent pyramidal shape of Mount Hood. In winter and spring, the mountain is especially magnificent, a sheet of white that turns pink and gold at sunset.

The old shops that purveyed clothing, shoes, and dry goods are mostly gone, replaced by painters, glass blowers, sculptors, guitar makers, restaurants, a boat builder, and a brewpub. It's a microcosm of the evolution of the small-town Northwest, from blue collar to white collar, from lumber to high tech and the arts, and an invigorating optimism pervades the place. With its flavor of the arts and the outdoors, it's like Hood River, right across the river, but on a smaller scale.

White Salmon and Bingen began as nineteenth-century farm towns. Later, steamboats on the river stopped at Bingen to pick up wood to fire their boilers and, as that trade declined, lumber mills thrived. Only one mill remains, SD&S Lumber in Bingen, but a new industry has arrived that has changed the area's face. It began in late 2002, when a company founded in 1994 by a couple of inventors in White Salmon developed a prototype of an unmanned aircraft. The United States invaded Iraq the next year, and the rest is the history of modern warfare. The company, Insitu, now employs over three hundred people and maintains operations in twelve buildings in White Salmon and Bingen. Insitu has brought money, new ideas, and a young, well-educated workforce, with an average age of thirty-nine. The environment keeps them there. They windsurf on the Columbia, fish the rivers and creeks of Klickitat County, ski Mt. Adams, and raft the White Salmon River.

The arrival of Insitu also revived local schools and gave a push to a community that had already begun to attract retirees, artisans, and entrepreneurs. Among the latter were David and Dennice Dierck, who purchased the Inn of the White Salmon, a brick building at the end of Jewett Boulevard, built in 1937. They are remodeling the place, gradually changing its décor from Victorian to a more sleek, modern look. The small lobby is furnished in themes of 1930s Americana and Victorian nostalgia but at each end of halls that branch from the lobby stand metal sculptures by John Mayo, a sculptor and industrial designer who works from a studio at the other end of Jewett Boulevard.

Visitors to White Salmon can spend hours on Jewett Boulevard, checking out the art and visiting with local artisans such as Ray Klebba, who owns White Salmon Boat Works. Klebba is in his sixties now and he's been building boats for some twenty years. He crafts his canoes, kayaks, and rowboats of strips of cedar glued together to form a light but strong shell. The sleek, gently curved watercraft are as much loved for their looks as for their performance on the water. Some of his clients float them, others use them as art objects—one even hung a canoe upside down over a breakfast bar. He also sells

179

boat plans and kits and accepts students for sixteen-day boat-building classes. Up the street is White Salmon Glassworks, a studio in a former grocery. Local artists use the furnaces and display their work there. Classes and play shops are also offered to kids and adults for making plates, tiles, and holiday ornaments. A few blocks down is the Hatcher Studio Arts building, which houses studios for six artists. John Mayo created the space, which also includes a computer lab and a metal-fabrication shop where he creates his skeletal metal sculptures. The studio offers no regular hours, but Mayo is usually in during the day.

The downtown arts scene offers only a sampling of the art produced in the area. Artists, attracted by the scenery and weather, hole up in houses and cabins tucked away in the forest off rural roads. Richard Schneider lives up a steep drive off Bates Road, announced by a sign for Gorge Metal Art and a metal sculpture of a lizard. Schneider is best known as Rooster, a name acquired when he lived for a time in a renovated chicken coop. He spends about half the year in the rustic-modern house that he built, creating metal sculptures and more utilitarian works like cable handrails. He also leads tours on the White Salmon River. In the winter, he heads for Mexico's Sierra Madre and the Copper Canyon where his Sierra Madre Motorcycle Adventures offers tours.

One way to experience the scenery around White Salmon is to take Washington 141 north. On the way, turn left down Eyrie Road and travel a mile or so to enjoy a view of the Gorge and Mount Hood. Continue on to BZ Corner and spend the rest of the afternoon tumbling down the White Salmon River in a rubber raft launched by Zoller's Outdoor Odysseys or one of the other rafting companies on the river. Zoller's eight-mile trips through steep basalt canyons take about two hours. With

180

any luck, Rooster will be your guide, completing a full circle of art and the outdoors in these parts.

The Basics: Inn of the White Salmon is an attractive hotel with a fine downtown location. Solstice Wood Fire Cafe in nearby Bingen is a pleasant place for lunch and dinner and the Ground Espresso Bar and Cafe down the street from the inn is a popular hangout.

Lyle

550

From the highway, Lyle is a scruffy place bunched up on the road and you are quickly through it. Above town, modern wooden houses hang at the edge of a bluff, capturing magnificent views of the river and of rock cliffs on the Oregon side. Down in town, it's flat and well used. River gentrification hasn't hit this place, and as a result it seems blue collar and close to the earth.

Lyle's drowsy appearance belies its heritage. For almost a century, it was wide awake. It began in the 1850s as Klickitat Landing and was later named for James Lyle, an early settler who became the postmaster. When water was the only highway in the Gorge, riverboats stopped at Lyle to drop off mail and load grain, animals, and fruits from Appleton, Goldendale, and points north. For years, until after World War II, the Lyle area also was one of the biggest producers of fattened lambs in the nation, and until the 1960s, sawmills in the vicinity added to the local payroll.

Present-day Lyle is much reduced, but the century-old Lyle Hotel is an asset that lots of small towns might envy. Coming into town from the west, turn right at Seventh Street. The hotel is a few blocks down, a beige two-story box of a place, hard edges softened by massive trees. Built originally in 1905 as a boarding house that served railroad workers, it closed in the late 1950s and sat abandoned for a couple of decades. The ten upstairs rooms, though nicely furnished, still reflect a place where working people occupied small spaces and depended on the transom window for ventilation.

Marianne Lewis and Steve Little, who were familiar as chefs on the Portland food scene in the 1980s, took over the hotel in 2009. Downstairs, the dining room has gone way beyond its roots. It's a place of long-stemmed wine glasses and white napery, without question the fanciest dining room in town. The hotel also offers a comfortable bar, but locals seem to prefer the Lyle Taproom, a welcoming, gently worn place where elderly customers drink beers and eat burgers and big bowls of hot soup. If the hotel bar is satin, the Taproom is flannel.

On a Saturday morning, Darrell England cooks breakfast at the Country Café on State Street. With his solemn face and salt-and-pepper beard, he looks like a pretty tough critter until he brings your coffee and sets it down with an unobtrusive, gentle movement. He came up from California a few years ago to fish and found plenty of opportunity. Rose Vanlaar owns the place. She ate there as a child and she has known her customers all her life. "A little mom and pop place," she calls it. The same could be said for the town. That morning, a couple of blocks away at the Fire Hall, a group gathered in a circle to brainstorm ways to deal with poverty in Lyle. For anyone who follows Northwest small towns, their problems and strategies, this was better than a James Bond movie. The town is unincorporated and volunteer groups like this one provide leadership and civic initiative.

183

If the town's prosperity has slid over the years, Lyle's position at the mouth of the Klickitat River remains one of the finest in the Gorge. The Lewis and Clark Expedition passed the river's mouth on October 29, 1805, and called it the Cataract River because natives told them of waterfalls upstream. From its source in the Cascades the Klickitat cuts ninety-five miles through basalt canyons to the Columbia. It's one of the longest undammed rivers in the Northwest, and ten miles of the river beginning at the confluence with the Columbia have been designated wild and scenic.

The curving, turbulent river offers some of the best salmon and steelhead fishing in the Gorge, and the Klickitat Trail has opened it to bikers and hikers. The trail starts at Lyle and follows the river thirty-one miles along the old railroad corridor. Even if you are not an angler, a hiker, or a biker, it's exciting to watch Yakama Nation fishermen, perched on platforms anchored in the river's rock walls, scoop salmon from the water with dipnets. Skilled dipnetters drag out one flopping fish after another and keep them for their own eating or sell them.

Lyle could remain as it is, a little town on the river with a past, but its environment guarantees that it will grow and change. A few miles up Washington 142 is Cor Cellars, a small winery owned by Luke Bradford, a transplant from New York City. He buys his grapes from Horse Heaven Hills in southeastern Washington and some also from vineyards in the Gorge, and produces twenty-five hundred cases, half red and half white. He was drawn to the Gorge by its scenery, climate, and recreation. Combining viniculture and river and mountain sports isn't unusual. By Bradford's estimation, half the twenty or so wineries in the Gorge are there because their owners loved the recreation.

184

The Lyle Hotel sells Cor Cellars wine but the Taproom doesn't. The Taproom at this writing was for sale, though, and the new owner may update the wine list, which is OK as long as an old-timer can get a bowl of soup.

The Basics: The Lyle Hotel is the only place to stay. Dinner is served in the dining room on Friday, Saturday, and Sunday, and bistro food is available in the bar Wednesday through Sunday. They also serve Saturday and Sunday brunch. The Country Café is good for breakfast and lunch.

Dayton

2,735

The Road: The best jumping-off point for Dayton is probably
the Tri Cities. Take Washington 124 from there and connect
with U.S. 12 at Waitsburg and continue east to Dayton. Another
route, coming from the north, let's say from Wenatchee, passes
through intriguing old towns such as the German-Russian
community of Odessa and numerous other farm towns in
varying degrees of picturesque decline.

Dayton sits in the wheat fields of southeastern Washington, established and confident, with a pedigree of history and money. Whatever the season, the wheat fields are mesmerizing, billowing over rolling hills to the horizon. Farms nestle in crinkles of hills and tiny hamlets emerge, sometimes in the company of an abandoned general store and a few other deteriorating buildings.

White settlers arrived in the area in the 1860s, drawn by weather and soil just right for growing wheat and other grains. In 1880, a visionary brewer, Jacob Weinhard, founded the Weinhard Brewery and later a malt house, saloon, theater, and bank. Fine homes dot the town, built in Queen Anne, Italianate, Gothic, and Craftsman styles and at least 117 residential and commercial buildings appear on the National Register of Historic Places. Dayton takes historic renovation seriously, and apparently the money is there to do it. The Dayton Historic Depot, built in 1881, is the oldest surviving train station in Washington and now is a museum. The Columbia County Courthouse, built in 1887, is the state's oldest functioning courthouse. A series of "modernizations" beginning in the 1930s had left the Italianate structure

185

stripped of its cupola and desecrated inside and out, but a restoration beginning in the mid-1980s returned the cupola to its place and brought the structure back to its original design. The town can also claim a restored theater, a polished hotel, and an excellent restaurant—unusual niceties for a little town on the prairie.

It's possible to spend a couple of days in Dayton, comfortably lodged, immersed in history, entertained, and well fed. The fifteen-room Weinhard Hotel inhabits the bones of a converted saloon and lodge hall that Weinhard built in 1890. It's about five minutes from the hotel to the Patit Creek Restaurant, a plain little house on the edge of town that carries a reputation for excellent food served in unpretentious surroundings. After dinner, guests can repair to the Liberty Theater on Main Street. The theater opened in 1910 but had sat vacant for almost thirty years until a local group began its restoration in 1994. It offers first-run and classic films and occasional live performances. A nightcap at Woody's Bar and Grill, a jolly place across the street from the hotel, would be a good way to end the evening.

For day touring, the Dayton Depot, now a museum, deserves a visit, and as a historic icon, it may be the most important place in town. Rail, which arrived in Dayton in 1880, transformed agriculture in Columbia County by offering access to national and international markets. I rate museums not by the size of the collection but by the presence of one or two evocative objects. In the Dayton Depot, it's a floral still life, pretty but unsettling, painted by a local artist, Jose Long Perkins. Perkins was born in Dayton in 1869 and married a traveling minister. The couple spent their married life on horseback, preaching from Washington to Montana. She was a talented artist, and her sister sent her art supplies on the road. The painting in the museum was Jose's last work. It has an aura of the grave—deep, melancholy colors, drooping leaves, a rendering of the poisonous castor bean. She committed suicide soon after completing it.

Waitsburg, nine miles away, is a museum of a different sort. You could stretch out for a nap on the sidewalk downtown and not be noticed—empty storefronts stare blindly where once there were two groceries, two hardware stores, three bars, two banks, two drugstores, a butcher, a saddle shop, a Chinese laundry, and a milliner. But the fine stone buildings remain largely intact, unspoiled by ambitions to bring them up to date with flimsy modern storefronts. Beyond the downtown, the street becomes an ideal of the nineteenth-century American small town, tree shaded and lined with commodious homes. One of the finest of these, aloof behind a cast-iron fence, is the Bruce Memorial Museum, built in 1883 as a residence for a local family. The museum's most telling display is a collection of women's hats, resting in a second-floor display case. They are extravagant creations of the time, rich with flowers, feathers, and furbelows. Two milliners maintained shops on Main Street, a luxurious amenity that's hard to imagine in the nearly deserted downtown.

187

The hats reflect a not-so-apparent reality of Waitsburg and Dayton. By outward appearances, these are not prosperous places. Columbia County's unemployment rate is chronically high compared to the rest of the state and Dayton is hardly a boutique community. Yet much of the money to restore Dayton's courthouse and the Liberty Theater was raised locally and several banks do business in town. Many of the local benefactors have lived in the area for generations. They dine at Patit Creek Restaurant and probably their grandmothers and great-grandmothers purchased hats in downtown Waitsburg.

The Basics: The Weinhard Hotel is the best place to stay for its comfort and downtown location. The Patit Creek Restaurant has become a regional institution for good reason. For a livelier, less-expensive dining experience, try Woody's Bar and Grill across the street from the Weinhard Hotel.

Epilogue

I cannot guarantee that all the people and places I mention in this book will be there in a year or so. Small towns only seem to operate in a time capsule. In fact there is continuous change: people die, businesses close, and items disappear from the menu.

Since I began visiting small Northwest towns regularly in 2000, lamentable things have happened. The defunct Paris Woolen Mill in Stayton, built in 1905 and jammed with idle looms and the machinery that ran them, was demolished in 2003. The Muir & McDonald Co. tannery in Dallas, the oldest operating business in Polk County, also has closed and it's only a matter of time before the rambling, decrepit building that housed it is torn down. The people of Imnaha no longer stage their annual Bear and Rattlesnake Feed, surely one of the most individual celebrations in Oregon. The news, however, is not altogether grim. Digger Don's in Sutherlin, which took its monster five-pound hamburger off the menu, has put it back; and the White Horse Saloon in McDermitt, which I once had described as a melancholy wreck, is undergoing a restoration.

Visible change seldom occurs overnight or even within a year or two. People move away, get sick, or die, not in a flood but a dribble. A town I won't name has over the last few years lost its hardware store, which was an anchor of Main Street, and two restaurants closed because few people could afford to eat in them. The business district recently was spiffed up with attractive benches and hanging flower baskets but there's almost no one downtown enjoying these amenities.

Despite gloomy forebodings, I don't think small towns in the Northwest will disappear, although some will surely become as spare and dried out as tumbleweed stuck on a

189

barbed wire fence. They may never recover the pride and optimism of the days when timber, fish, and wheat made them self sufficient, but the most striking quality I find in these places isn't deterioration but resilience. Chambers of Commerce are everywhere and downtown improvement organizations spring up. Residents throw themselves into the public life of towns that are held together by voluntarism.

Entrepreneurs open new businesses in towns that look like the electricity is about to be turned off—new brewpubs, for example, have opened in Oakridge and White Salmon, old hotels have been remodeled in Union, Lyle, Toledo, and Willamina. Fine city parks are created or improved in places like Depoe Bay, Oakridge, Rainier, and Rogue River.

Almost all small towns are blessed with an amenity that makes residents feel good and inspires newcomers to settle in them. That's their natural surroundings, and no one can pull the plug on that. From any place in town, people see nature pressing up against the edges: surging rivers, forested mountains, brushy hills, wheat fields, rocky desert, the Pacific Ocean. Towns like Myrtle Point, Fossil, Merlin, Cathlamet, Lakeview, Jordan Valley, Oakridge, and dozens of others carry on daily life in view of spectacular surroundings. The last mill in the lumber town of Powers, high in Oregon's Coast Range, closed in the early 1970s but the town is still alive and breathing. There are dreams for the place, and people aren't giving up. And if you stand on the main street when the late afternoon light brushes the forested mountains that plunge down to the town, you understand the reason.

190

Index

For list of towns in the book, see the table of contents

annual events:
  Buster Keaton Day (Cottage Grove), 37
  community yard sale (Powers), 68
  crab feed (Charleston), 62
  crab feed (Elgin), 149
  crab feed (Halfway), 62, 152
  folk music festival (Toledo), 66
  Linn County Pioneer Picnic (Brownsville), 10
  Mosquito Festival (Paisley), 98
  Muddy Frogwater Festival (Milton-Freewater), 136
  Mule Days (Fossil), 114

Bagby Hot Springs, 13
Black Cap Mountain, 102

Cape Arago Lighthouse, 62
Cape Lookout, 51
Cape Meares Lighthouse, 51
cemeteries:
  Gardiner, 58
  Gold Beach pioneer, 70
  Miller Cemetery Church (Mt. Angel), 19
  Old Pioneer (Milton-Freewater), 138
  Prairie (Prairie City), 130
  Vila pioneer (Estacada), 15
Charbonneau grave (Jordan Valley), 155-56
cider tasting, 137
courthouses:
  Columbia County (WA), 185
  Grant County (OR), 125
  Morrow County (OR), 116
  Pacific County (WA), 172
  Polk County (OR), 20
  Sherman County (OR), 111
  Wallowa County (OR), 143
  Wheeler County (OR), 113

Fort McDermitt Indian Reservation, 162

Harney County Fairgrounds, 159
Hart Mountain Antelope Refuge, 103
Hidden Creek Watershed Trail, 62

John Day Fossil Beds, 112, 127

Lucky Strike Mine, 124

Morrow County Agricultural Collection, 116
Mount Angel Abbey, 17-18 *Mary D Hume* (Gold Beach), 71
museums:
  Bruce Memorial Museum (Waitsburg), 187
  Columbia Pacific Heritage Museum (Ilwaco), 175
  Coos County Fairgrounds (Myrtle Point), 65
  Cottage Grove Museum (Cottage Grove), 36
  Dayton Historic Depot (Dayton), 185
  DeWitt Museum (Prairie City), 130
  Eagle Cap Excursion Train (Elgin), 148
  Elgin Museum Historical Society (Elgin), 148
  Fort Rock Valley Historical Homestead Museum (Christmas Valley), 96
  Fossil Museum (Fossil), 113
  Frazier Farmstead Museum (Milton-Freewater), 138
  Grant County Historical Museum (Canyon City), 127
  Harney County Historical Museum (Burns), 159
  Harrisburg Area Museum (Harrisburg), 33
  Kam Wah Chung Museum (John Day), 127
  Linn County Historical Museum (Brownsville), 27

Marsh's Free Museum (Long Beach), 175
Morrow County Museum (Heppner), 117
Moyer House (Brownsville), 27
Oakridge Museum (Oakridge), 40
Pine Valley Community Museum (Halfway), 152
Polk County Museum (Dallas), 22
Reorganized Church of Jesus Christ of Latter Day Saints (logging museum) (Myrtle Point), 65
Schminck Memorial Museum (Lakeview), 104
Sherman County Historical Museum (Moro), 110
Spray Pioneer Museum (Spray), 119
Sumpter Municipal Museum (Sumpter), 133
Tillamook County Pioneer Museum (Garibaldi), 15, 48, 49
Trail Creek Tavern Museum (Shady Cove), 88
Wanger House (Powers), 68
Woodinville Museum (Rogue River), 84
music and theaters:
Asleep at the Switch (Garibaldi), 50
Elgin Opera House (Elgin), 148
Fossil Players, 113
Moonfall Theater (Dallas), 21
Oasis Lounge (Reedsport), 60
ZCBJ hall (Scio), 26

Oregon Caves, 90
Oregon Vortex, 85

parks and gardens:
Cape Disappointment State Park (Ilwaco), 174-75
Casey State Park (Shady Cove), 88
Dallas City Park, 21
Great Cats World Park (Cave Junction), 90
Greenwaters Park (Oakridge), 39
Harris County Park (Milton-Freewater), 137
Palmerton Arboretum (Rogue River), 83
Prehistoric Gardens (Gold Beach), 72
Riverfront Park (Harrisburg), 33
Three Arch Rocks National Wildlife Refuge (Oceanside), 51
Wenaha-Tucannon Wilderness (Troy), 140

river rafting:
Estacada, 14
Shady Cove, 87-88;
Spray, 120
Troy, 140
White Salmon, 179

scenic byways:
High Desert Discovery, 159
Journey Through Time, 139
West Cascade National, 39
South Slough Estuarine Reserve (Charleston), 62

Umpqua River Lighthouse, 59

Wahkiakum Ferry (Clatskanie), 46

zorses (Christmas Valley), 96

192